BRAGG
APPLE CIDER
VINEGAR
MIRACLE HEALTH SYSTEM

with the

BRAGG HEALTHY LIFESTYLE
Blueprint for Physical, Mental and Spiritual
Improvement . . .Healthy, Vital Living to 120
Genesis 6:3

PAUL C. BRAGG, N.D., Ph.D.
LIFE EXTENSION SPECIALIST
and
PATRICIA BRAGG, N.D., Ph.D.
HEALTH & FITNESS EXPERT

Health   *Peace*

Happiness   *Youthfulness*

Love   *Joy*

Praise   *Patience*

Vitality   *Fortitude*

Strength   *Charity*

Faith

JOIN   W9-AAC-225

The Bragg Crusades for a 100% Healthy, Better World for All!

HEALTH SCIENCE
Box 7, Santa Barbara, CA 93102 USA
World Wide Web: http://www.bragg.com

BRAGG
APPLE CIDER
VINEGAR
MIRACLE HEALTH SYSTEM

PAUL C. BRAGG, N.D., Ph.D.
LIFE EXTENSION SPECIALIST
and
PATRICIA BRAGG, N.D., Ph.D.
HEALTH & FITNESS EXPERT

Health Science, Box 7, Santa Barbara, California, 93102.
Telephone (805) 968-1020, FAX (805) 968-1001

**To order Bragg Books and products on-line, visit our
World Wide Web site at: http://www.bragg.com**

Quantity Purchases: Companies, Professional Groups, Churches, Clubs, etc. please contact our Special Sales Department.

- REVISED -
Copyright © Health Science

Forty-sixth printing MCMXCV
ISBN: 0-87790-029-9

Published in the United States
HEALTH SCIENCE   Box 7, Santa Barbara, Calif. 93102 USA

PAUL C. BRAGG, N.D., Ph.D.
World's leading authorithy
❧ on Healthy Lifestyle Living! ❧

JOIN THE FUN AT THE BRAGG "LONGER LIFE, HEALTH & HAPPINESS CLUB" WHEN YOU VISIT HAWAII – IT'S FREE!

Paul C. Bragg, daughter Patricia and their wonderful healthy members of the Bragg "Longer Life, Health and Happiness Club" exercise daily at the beautiful Fort DeRussy lawn, at the world famous Waikiki Beach in Honolulu, Hawaii. Membership is free and open to everyone who wishes to attend any morning – Monday through Saturday, from 9 to 10:30 am for Bragg Deep Breathing exercises and exercises for health and fitness. Often on Saturday there are health lectures on how to live a long, healthy life! The group averages 75 to 125 per day, according to the seasons. From December to March it can go up to 200. When away lecturing, their dedicated leaders carry on until their return. Thousands have visited the club from around the world and then carry the message of health and fitness to friends and relatives back home. Patricia extends an invitation to you and your friends to join the club for wholesome, healthy fellowship . . . when you visit Honolulu, Hawaii. Be sure also to visit the outer Hawaiian Islands (Maui, Kauai, Hawaii, Molokai) for a fulfilling, healthy vacation.

To maintain good health the body must be exercised properly (stretching, walking, jogging, running, biking, swimming, deep breathing, good posture, etc.) and nourished wisely (natural foods), so to maintain a normal weight and increase the good life of radiant health, joy & happiness. – Paul C. Bragg

KEEP YOUNG BIOLOGICALLY
WITH EXERCISE AND GOOD NUTRITION

You can always remember that you have the following good reasons for sticking to your health program:

- The ironclad laws of Mother Nature and God.
- Your common sense which tells you that you are doing right.
- Your aim to make your health better and your life longer.
- Your resolve to prevent illness so that you may enjoy life to the fullest.
- By making an art of healthy living, you will be young at any age.
- You will retain your faculties and be hale, hearty, active and useful far beyond the ordinary length of years, and you will also possess superior mental, emotional and physical powers.

WANTED - For Robbing Health & Life

KILLER Saturated Fats	*CHOKER Hydrogenated Fats*
CLOGGER Salt	*DEADEYED Devitalized Foods*
DOPEY Caffeine	*HARD (Inorganic Minerals) Water*
PLUGGER Frying Pan	*CRAZY Alcohol*
DEATH-DEALER Drugs	*SMOKEY Tobacco*
JERKEY Turbulent Emotions	*LOAFER Laziness*
GREASY Overweight	*HOGGY Over-Eating*

What Wise Men Say

Wisdom does not show itself so much in precept as in life - a firmness of mind and mastery of appetite.   – Seneca

Govern well thy appetite, lest Sin surprise thee and her attendant Death.   – Milton

Our prayers should be for a sound mind in a healthy body.   – Juvenal

Health consists with Temperance alone. – Pope

Health is . . . a blessing that money cannot buy.   – Izaak Walton

I saw few die of hunger - of eating, a hundred-thousand.   – Ben Franklin

Let nature be your teacher.   – Wordsworth

The natural healing force within us is the greatest force in getting well.
– Hippocrates, Father of Medicine

Of all the knowledge, that most worth having is knowledge about health.
The first requisite of a good life is to be a healthy person. – Herbert Spencer

CONTENTS

In 400 B.C., Hippocrates, the Father of Medicine, treated his patients with amazing apple cider vinegar for its powerful healing and cleansing qualities. It is a naturally occurring antibiotic and antiseptic.

BRAGG CRUSADES For The 1990s
Teaching People World-Wide To Live
Healthier, Stronger Lives For A Better World

We love sharing, teaching and giving and you can share this love by being part of Bragg Crusades World-Wide Outreach. Bragg Crusades is dedicated to helping others. We feel blessed when your life improves from our teachings in the Bragg Books and Crusades. It makes our years of service so worthwhile!

The Miracle of Fasting book has been the No. 1 book for 10 years now in Russia. Why? Because we show them how to live a healthy, wholesome life for less money, and it's so easy to understand and follow. Most healthful lifestyle habits are free (examples - deep breathing, exercise, clean thoughts, good posture and plain, natural foods). We are continuing with all our health teachings, lectures, Crusades, radio, TV and video outreaches to reach the multitudes.

My joy and priorities come from God and healthy living. I'm excited about spreading health world-wide, for now it's needed more than ever. My father and I were also TV Health Pioneers, with our program "Health and Happiness" filmed in Hollywood. It's thrilling to be a Health Crusader and you will enjoy it also.

By reading the Bragg Self-Health Books you can also gain a new confidence that you are helping yourself, family & friends to Healthy Principles of Living! Please call your local health store & book store and ask for the Bragg Books. We hope to have all the stores stock the Bragg Books so they will be available to all.

I have visions of **Health Retreats** where people can find radiant health, joy and rebirth! They **will be Recharging - Physically, Mentally, Emotionally and Spiritually.** I was reared on Retreats ... holidays and vacations were spent at Camp for precious weeks of growth and recharge. You'll love them, too!

For the 1990s, we are planning Bragg Recharge Retreats, also Child & Senior Care Centers which are desperately needed across America. We are just waiting for the right locations and funding. We can accept all gifts, monetary and land (appraised value), and we can give a receipt for tax deductions. We could develop seldom-used ranches, farms and old estates into Recharge Centers for rejuvenating mind, body and soul. Those attending would become health crusaders for their families and friends. Empty buildings and spacious older homes with yards would make ideal Child & Senior Care Centers. Those who have any locations and who would like to be part of this great outreach, please write to me.

We are not new to retreats; my Dad pioneered the first health spa (Macfadden's Deauville) in Miami Beach and others in Highland Springs, CA and Danville, NY.

I expend all my energy and funds helping others to help themselves! Genuine love seeks ways to express itself! I thank you for your caring, sharing, support. For with your help we can achieve our goals for the 1990s. I know God will bless you. Your needed help will be a blessing to the Bragg Crusades. Our 1990s budget is for a mighty worthwhile cause. I know you, your family and friends will enjoy and benefit from the teachings and retreats.

With A Loving, Grateful Heart,

BRAGG CRUSADES, America's Health Pioneers
A non-profit charitable organization. Gifts are tax deductible.
7340 Hollister Ave., Santa Barbara, CA 93117 USA (805) 968-1020
Over 80 continuous years spreading health and fitness worldwide.

HOW TO USE
POWERFUL HEALTH QUALITIES OF
NATURAL APPLE CIDER VINEGAR

Natural (undistilled) apple cider vinegar (ACV) can really be called one of nature's most perfect foods,* and is made from fresh crushed organic apples and then allowed to mature. It's best matured in wooden barrels, as wood seems to "boost" the natural fermentation. Natural ACV should be a rich brownish color and if held to the light you might see a tiny formation of cob-web-like substances which we call the "mother." The more matured the ACV, usually some "mother" will show in the bottom of the bottle. You can save some mother and transfer it to work in other vinegar bottles. When you smell natural ACV there should be a pungent odor, and some are so natural and ripened they pucker your mouth.

WHY HAS NATURAL, FULLY AGED
APPLE CIDER VINEGAR ALMOST
DISAPPEARED FROM GROCERS' SHELVES?

The blame for the disappearance of natural apple cider vinegar from supermarkets lies on the shoulders of the general public, as well as the producers of vinegar.

Most people buy food with their eyes and not their knowledge of nutrition. The vinegar producers failed to enlighten the public on what powerful health qualities were locked within natural ACV . . . Why? Because most of them had not the *slightest* knowledge of the health values of apple cider vinegar. They produced vinegar because the public demanded it. It was simply filling supply and demand.

A teacher for the day can be guiding lights for a lifetime!
Bragg books are silent health teachers - never tiring, ready night or day to help you help yourself to health! Our books are written with love and a deep desire to guide you to healthy living.   – Patricia Bragg

---

* The best is our organic, raw, unfiltered, unpasteurized apple cider vinegar, available in most Health Stores. See back pages for details.

POWERFUL HEALTH QUALITIES REMOVED

You cannot completely blame the producers of vinegar. They are not nutritionists, nor are they biochemists. Their business is to give the customers what they want.

Most people purchase vinegar for flavoring their foods. Some women purchase it to rinse their hair after shampooing, as it makes the hair soft and easier to manage. Some purchase it to put in water to wash windows, also it's a great deodorizer. Both the general public and the producers of vinegar have been in total darkness as to the powerful health qualities of natural, fully ripened apple cider vinegar. Ignorance isn't always bliss. When most people see natural apple cider vinegar with the dark color and the dark, cob-web *mother* floating in it, they think it looks unappetizing. The general public has been educated and brainwashed to want everything they purchase to have perfect eye appeal!

To meet this demand that vinegar must be bright colored and free from the dark cob-web *mother* – this is the reason producers distill the vinegar. In distilling, the vinegar is turned to steam by heating, therefore destroying the powerful enzymes and distilling out the powerful life-giving minerals such as: potassium, phosphorus, natural organic sodium, magnesium, sulphur, iron, copper, natural organic fluorine, silicon and many other powerful trace minerals! Distilling also destroys the powerful natural malic acid which is so very important in fighting body toxins.

You can plainly see how the general public, with their obsession for *eye appeal foods*, react. The producers of apple cider vinegar, who agreed to sell their product for a profit, put a death warrant against healthy, natural fully ripened ACV. The public got just what they wanted – beautiful, but dead ACV. When natural ACV was hard to find, other strange vinegars began to appear on grocery shelves. The first was malt vinegar, a refined, processed vinegar. It's clear, white-looking and acceptable to the public. Though it tastes like vinegar, it has none of the qualities of natural ACV.

Then came the real tragedy: some food chemist produced an imitation vinegar from coal tar. It looked white, pure and it tasted like vinegar. Now, this is the biggest seller of all vinegars in supermarkets. It is cheaper than distilled vinegar or malt vinegar. Today most people purchase this synthetic vinegar. There is not much that is positive to say about it, except that it is pretty and it tastes like vinegar, but it has absolutely no health value!

So, here we have three commercial types of vinegar on the general market. They don't contain the nutritional and health values of natural, fully ripened apple cider vinegar. Millions of people around the world never get the health qualities of wholesome, natural apple cider vinegar.

MILLIONS SUFFER FROM MAL-NUTRITION

"Mal" means bad. As a consequence of not getting natural, healthy, balanced diets, millions around the world suffer from many forms of sub-clinical mal-nutrition. This means that many people, due to vitamin and mineral deficiencies, feel half-sick most of the time. They lack vim, vigor and the "Go Power" to carry on the ordinary duties of life without feeling tired most of the time. Their daily food intake and the commercial vinegars they use do not provide them with the proper number of vitamins, minerals and potassium their bodies require. They lack important vital power! They drag themselves through the day feeling exhausted most of the time. This is the reason they turn to stimulants such as: coffee, tea, cola drinks, alcohol and cigarettes, over-the-counter drugs and even to dangerous drugs that "pep" them up for a while. After the effects of these stimulants wear off, they feel terrible. They just exist, and are not living full, happy, healthy lives!

You see these unhappy people about you every day. They are *washed-out* and ageing prematurely. They often lack skin and muscle tone. They have dark circles and puff (water) bags under their eyes. Their eyes lose the sparkle of health and youthfulness and become like *dead fish eyes*. Mal-nourished people are mostly lifeless and everything they do requires a tremendous effort. They are not really living and most are not happy. Many suffer from depression and mental fatigue.

The Doctor of the future will give no medicine but will interest his patients in the care of the human frame, in diet and in the cause and prevention of disease. —Thomas A. Edison

APPLES ARE POWERFUL NUTRITIONAL FOODS

"An apple a day keeps the doctor away" is a familiar saying known to millions. This carries truth and good common sense, because the apple is one of God's great health-giving foods.

Apples are a rich source of potassium, which is to the soft tissues of the body what calcium is to the bones and harder tissues. Potassium is the mineral of youthfulness; it is the "artery softener," keeping the arteries of the body flexible and resilient. It is a fighter of dangerous bacteria and viruses. Yes, when you say "An apple a day keeps the doctor away," you are talking good down-to-earth vital nutrition.

The apple has stood the test of time. It is one of the oldest fruits that man consumes. It was in the garden of Eden that the apple played such a vital part in man's destiny. Man has been an apple eater for thousands of years. Apple eaters have a certain healthfulness that non-apple eaters never achieve.

APPLES – RICH IN POTASSIUM, MINERALS AND ENZYMES

While the apple is a delicious fruit and most people enjoy eating apples, we look on the apple as more than something good to eat. Potassium is the key mineral in the constellation of minerals, and is so important to the life of every living thing, for without it there would be no life!

Most humans are deficient in potassium and it reflects in their cell tissues and their entire body. Look about you... how many people do you see that have the super glow of health?

Millions living in today's civilization and eating the commercialized, processed foods available have a potassium deficiency look. The skin and muscle tone is bad. The flesh does not cling firm on the body's boney framework. Lines and wrinkles fill the face and neck and flabby skin hangs over the eyes. The longer the potassium deficiency continues, this prolapsing eyelid progresses. Soon people are looking out of little slits, instead of wide-open eyes. Thousands have turned to eye-lift surgery to correct hooded eyelids. Of course, the average person blames this on the fact that they have been adding more birthdays to their life. Most people attribute physical changes in the skin and muscle tone to their age.

You must have potassium to build and maintain youthful, ageless tissues. If you do not get your required amount of potassium daily, you acquire an *old age look*. This is premature ageing due to potassium deficiency.

It is the same in your flower and vegetable garden. Potassium is necessary to the production of the substances which give rigidity to plant stems and increase their resistance to the many diseases which attack plants. Potassium is also the powerful element which changes seeds into plants and flowers by progressive development. If plants become deficient in potassium, they stop their evolution at some intermediate stage. The first sign of extreme potassium deficiency is cessation of growth for no discernible external reason. If the potassium deficiency is not corrected, the plant slowly starts to wither, turns yellow and dies. The same with an animal and a human body; when there is a potassium deficiency, there is a slow degeneration of body cells.

REFINED, PROCESSED FOODS REMOVE VITAL POTASSIUM, INCREASING POOR HEALTH AND DISEASE

Robbed grains: The miller refines and processes our grains to get white flour which will keep for years. No vermin will eat it because it has been robbed of its potassium.

Amazing potassium loss in making white flour: In milling wheat the miller refines out 25 important food elements, amino acids, vitamin E, bran, the rich B-complex vitamins and entirely refines out the potassium. Cows fed refined grain, with the potassium milled out and de-germed, died early of heart failure.

The more we refine potassium out of foods, the sicker we get: People are spending and wasting time, money and energy on more sickness! The #1 plan should be to educate Americans about eating and living habits for super nutrition and superior health . . . promoting bones that last a lifetime, cells that resist disease and arteries that stay healthy and cholesterol-free.

Every man is the builder of a temple called his body . . . We are all sculptors and painters, and our material is our own flesh and blood and bones. Any nobleness begins at once to refine a man's features, any meanness or sensual to imbrute them.   – Henry David Thoreau

THE #1 CAUSE OF SICKNESS IS BAD NUTRITION

People don't die of infectious conditions as such, but it's malnutrition that allows the germs to gain a foothold in malnourished bodies. Also in non-infectious, fatal or degenerative conditions, bad nutrition is usually the main cause.

When the body has its full vitamin and mineral quota, including precious potassium, it is impossible for germs to get a foothold in a healthy, powerful bloodstream and body.

THE BODY HAS A SEED OF ETERNAL LIFE

Outside of fatal accidents, there is no reason why a man should leave before his time. It has been proven by some of the greatest scientific minds that there are no special diseases of old age. A person should not die simply because they live to 60, 70, 80, or 90 years of age, because calendar age is not toxic. Man creates his toxins by his eating and living habits.

Most people die of some fatal condition that they have built into their bodies by incorrect living or by violating or not knowing the natural laws that govern the physical body.

The two great enemies of life are toxic poisons (found in food, air, water and soil) and nutritional deficiencies caused by improper diet and unhealthy foods. The best prevention of sickness is to eat vital, healthy foods . . . especially potassium. These provide the body with correct, life-giving nourishment.

Every 90 days a new bloodstream ,the river of life, is built in the body by the food you eat, the liquid you drink and the air you breathe. From the bloodstream the body cells are made, nourished and maintained. Every 11 months we have a new set of billions of miraculous body cells, and every 7 years we have an entirely new set of bones and hard tissues.

There is nothing to get old – no ageing in the constantly renewing cells and body . . . your precious home for life.

Every day the average heart, your best friend, beats 100,000 times and pumps 2,000 gallons of blood for nourishing your body. In 70 years that adds up to more than 360 million (faithful) heartbeats. Please be good to your heart and live the Bragg Healthy Lifestyle for a long, happy, healthy life! . . . Here's to Genesis 6:3 for you. – Patricia Bragg

DR. ALEXIS CARREL'S GREAT EXPERIMENT

In his famous experiment of 1912 in New York City, Dr. Alexis Carrel *kept the cells of an embryo chicken heart alive and in health for over 30 years by daily monitoring the complete nutrition, cleansing and elimination.* The normal life-span of a chicken is 7 1/2 to 8 years.

Apple cider vinegar was given to the chicken embryo daily for its full quota of potassium. Dr. Carrel definitely proved to the entire world that the body has a seed of eternal life, for he could have continued this experiment indefinitely to give the embryo eternity, but felt 30 years proved the point . . . that man kills himself by his wrong habits of eating and living. This experiment showed to us the importance of apple cider vinegar to life, health and longevity.

The results revealed the key to total health and longevity. Many scientists know no reason why these same principles could not apply to human beings.

POTASSIUM DEFICIENCY CAN STUNT GROWTH

We have made over 10 scientific nutritional expeditions throughout the primitive world studying the growth of various races of people. We found areas where the top-soil was deficient in potassium and the people living off food grown from this potassium deficient soil were prone to be stunted in growth and have a shorter life-span.

The pygmies of Africa are stunted and short-lived. The same is true of the Arctic Eskimos . . . they just do not get in their daily diet the required amount of potassium and other minerals important to growth, health and long life.

MENTALLY RETARDED CHILDREN AND ADULTS SUFFER FROM POTASSIUM DEFICIENCY

We have closely studied the relationship between mentally retarded children and adults and potassium deficiency.

Many years ago, my dad brought three mentally retarded children to our home for study and observation. Each morning the children had the ACV cocktail (1 teaspoon ACV with a teaspoon raw honey, both rich potassium sources). Dad put the children on the Bragg Healthy Lifestyle, that gave them extra amounts of wonderful potassium. Daily they were

7

given vitamin-mineral supplements and some Niacin (50 mgs – vitamin B-3). In three weeks these children became more mentally alert, and after keeping them in our home for almost a year they were able to resume their schooling with children of their own age.

At another time we brought three mentally retarded adults into our home and by giving them the ACV routine enabled them to become self-supporting in less than a year.

EXERCISES HELP KEEP YOU
YOUTHFUL, FLEXIBLE AND TRIM

see page 60

Paul C. Bragg and friend, Roy White, 106 years young
They both practiced progressive weight training 3 times a week for staying healthy and fit. Scientists have proven that weight training works miracles for all ages in maintaining flexibility, energy and youthful stamina.

SENILITY AND POTASSIUM DEFICIENCY

Throughout the world, there are millions of prematurely old, senile people. They are the forgotten people. Many of them do not know their own name, nor can they recognize their family or closest friends. They are just living human vegetables. Old senile people are the most pitiful people on earth. They are just existing. Some of them have so degenerated that it's hopeless to try and salvage them.

However, we believe that many of them can be restored to useful lives again if the toxic poisons are flushed from their bodies and their grave nutritional deficiencies are corrected!

Years ago we selected four senile people who we felt could be helped. We put them on the Bragg Healthy Lifestyle, with healthy foods rich in potassium and ACV cocktails. Out of the four, we were able to salvage three of them. All three left the convalescent home they had been confined in and became healthy, happy and self-sufficient. Two of them made a remarkable recovery . . . one went back to contracting and building at 83 years young, and the other resumed his accounting career in his mid 80's. (See example pages 60-61.)

Most senile people suffer from a clogged arterial system. Potassium is to the soft tissues of the body what calcium is to the hard structures of the body. The potassium goes into the clogged, caked arteries and cleans out the rust and dirt . . . just like vinegar water removes grime from windows. One can't think clearly if the arteries are heavily clogged with cholesterol and toxic poisons.

Potassium might be called the great detergent of the arteries. There is little doubt that potassium slows up the hardening and clogging processes that menace the whole important cardiovascular system. Natural, ripened apple cider vinegar contains the miraculous potassium that makes the flesh of farm animals healthier and more tender (see pages 11 snd 26). There is very little doubt that one of the functions of potassium is to keep the tissues healthy, soft and pliable, whether it be animal or man.

It's never too late to begin getting into shape, but it does take daily perseverance.   *– Thomas K. Cureton*

Aches and pains in the bones and muscles, especially in lower back.

Shooting pains when a person starts to straighten up after leaning over.

Dizziness upon straightening up after leaning over.

A dull morning headache upon arising.

The body feels heavy and it's an effort to move rapidly.

The hair is dull, faded looking, lacks lustre and sheen.

The scalp is itchy, and dandruff and premature hair-thinning or balding may occur.

 The hair is unmanageable, mats up and often looks like straw. Sometimes it's extremely dry, and other times it feels like it's oil soaked.

The eyes itch and feel sore. Sometimes the eyelids are granulated and white matter collects at the corners. At other times the eyes are bloodshot and watery.

The eyes tire easily and will not focus as they should.

There is a loss of mental alertness, making decisions difficult to make. The memory seems to fail, making you forget names and places that should be at the tip of your tongue. You become very forgetful.

 You tire physically and mentally with the slightest effort.

You become impatient and sometimes very irritable with your family and loved ones, and even with your business and social acquaintances.

 You feel nervous and have periods of depression and mental fog. You have difficulty getting things done, due to mental and muscle fatigue. The slightest effort sometimes leaves you shaking and trembling.

At times the hands and the feet get chilled and cold, even in warm weather.

PAUL C. BRAGG TALKS ABOUT USES OF
APPLE CIDER VINEGAR ON HIS FAMILY'S FARM

Long years of research have proven to me that natural apple cider vinegar (ACV) is a potent source of potassium.

I was raised on a large farm. On this farm we grew many varieties of apples. I was a great apple eater. In my early youth I enjoyed robust health. Each year my father made natural ACV and stored it in wooden barrels. On our table we used this natural ACV and our large family loved it.

My father was a splendid farmer and many times I would watch him add ACV to the feed and water of ailing animals (cattle, horses, sheep, dogs, cats, etc.) and it acted like magic. The ACV seemed to possess some miracle ingredient that could help restore health to the animals.* See example pg. 26

*Apple Cider Vinegar dosage for sick animals: Acute cases double this dosage. 1/2 teaspoon small animals, 1 teaspoon large animals, twice daily in feed or water. Optional: mix ACV with 1/4 cup water, place into mouth with squeeze bottle or baster.

The nearest doctor was 32 miles from our home. If a doctor was needed, he had to come by horse and buggy over miles of rough, dirt roads. So, at our home we developed simple self-health remedies and ACV played an important health role.

I well remember when my father put in long hours at the farm work during the harvest period. He was up long before day break and would not retire until late at night. I would watch him come into our kitchen, put a heaping teaspoon of honey in a glass, then add 2 teaspoons of pure ACV, then fill the glass with water and sip it slowly!

I would say *Father, why do you drink vinegar, honey and water?* And father would reply, *Son, farm work is long hard work, it can produce chronic fatigue in the body. Whatever is in this mixture relieves me of that chronic fatigue.*

Yes, father was correct. There was an ingredient in that drink that renewed his vitality and relieved him of chronic fatigue and stiffness, that ingredient is potassium, along with its powerful enzymes that are found in ACV.

Most people today when they work hard, turn to all kinds of dangerous stimulants to relieve their chronic fatigue: alcohol, tobacco, coffee, tea, cola-soft drinks, pep pills and even dangerous, addictive drugs.

My father's good advice fell on youthful ears. It was some years later that I realized that my father was a smart man in using raw honey and ACV to combat chronic fatigue.

At 12, I was sent from my rugged farm life to an expensive military academy . . . a gift for saving a man from drowning. The food at that institution was where my health was broken. The refined, overcooked and processed food broke my health and made me a victim of that consuming disease, tuberculosis. At no time did I see our wonderful apple cider vinegar or honey at the table of our military academy. It was not until I met the great Dr. Rollier at his sanitarium in Switzerland, where I regained my health, that I again came in contact with the many miracles of apple cider vinegar and honey . . . both of which are so rich in essential potassium.

I owe much of my recovery to ACV and honey as it is a hard fighter against germs and toxins. At the sanitarium I was given each morning the same drink my father took for energy and health. Dr. Rollier urged us to put ACV on our raw vegetable salads and steamed greens. He also urged us to use an abundance each day of fresh raw vegetables and fresh fruits as they are nature's purifiers. He was a wise doctor and knew how valuable potassium and raw fruits and vegetables were to maintaining health of the body chemistry.

I was 100% cured from TB in less than two years after benefiting from a perfectly balanced natural diet, correct deep breathing and alpine sunshine. Healthy living was my cure. I have also been an ardent user of ACV and honey ever since and in our Bragg health teachings and writings advocate the use of this miracle source of potassium.

It was in Switzerland that I started to fulfill my earlier pledge to God . . . if I recovered my health, I would become a health crusader and devote my life to sharing the message of health and wellness with the world! When I finished my schooling, I went on to full-time crusading for a healthier world! I founded the health movement and originated and named the first health food store. Then, through my health crusades, I inspired hundreds of Bragg students to open the first health food stores in their areas across America and around the world. *Everyday was a joy for me – sharing health.*

APPLE CIDER VINEGAR FOR OVERWEIGHT

We want it understood that ACV will not reduce a person who does not control their intake of food. But, when combined with a diet of 1,000 to 1,200 calories daily, it will assist in reducing excess weight. The Diet Research Center in England reported: *better reducing and firming with ACV daily massages - mixture of 3 parts ACV to 1 part almond or olive oil - helps the body rid excess fat.* The ACV and honey cocktail should be taken 3 times daily. It consists of 1/2 tsp honey plus 1 tsp ACV in a glass of distilled water at room temperature.

Along with this ACV health cocktail there must be exercise and a reducing diet. (Read the *Bragg Reducing Book* and the *Miracle of Fasting* for more reducing information.) That means that all refined, processed, sugared products and beverages, and all dairy products are eliminated from the diet. The diet should consist of a wide variety of fresh fruits; raw salads; raw, steamed, baked or wokked vegetables; brown rice; tofu; beans; and whole grain pastas. Read our two Bragg Health Recipe Books for hundreds of delicious and healthy recipes. Our books are available at most health food stores. If unavailable, see back pages for ordering.

COMBATING UNDERWEIGHT

Apple cider vinegar is proving to be one of the greatest aids to health known to science, and it's an entirely natural substance, produced by powerful natural enzymes.

The underweight person is usually deficient in these powerful enzymes and therefore cannot use or burn up the food that is put into the body. No matter how much fatty food, protein or any other kind of food ingested, most often it is not utilized by the body, if important enzymes are missing.

Enzyme deficiencies always cause problems! The underweight person should use the following ACV cocktail upon arising: 1 tsp ACV and 1 tsp honey in a glass of distilled water. Add to this 2 drops of liquid iodine made from seaweed, available in health stores. This adds natural iodine which is so important to body health, and helps normalize body weight up or down as needed. Then with each meal take a multi-digestive enzyme, and always be faithful to the Bragg Healthy Lifestyle. Remember, healthy food is needed body fuel.

13

BENEFITS FROM THE JOYS OF FASTING

Fasting is easier than any diet. • Fasting is the quickest way to lose weight.
Fasting is adaptable to a busy life. • Fasting gives the body a physiological rest.
Fasting is used successfully in the treatment of many physical illnesses.
Fasting can yield weight losses of up to 10 pounds or more in the first week.
Fasting lowers & normalizes cholesterol and blood pressure levels.
Fasting is a calming experience, often relieving tension and insomnia.
Fasting improves dietary habits. • Fasting increases eating pleasure.
Fasting frequently induces feelings of euphoria, a natural *high*.
Fasting is a rejuvenator, slowing the ageing process.
Fasting is an energizer, not a debilitator. • Fasting aids the elimination process.
Fasting often results in a more vigorous sex life.
Fasting can eliminate or modify smoking, drug and drinking addictions.
Fasting is a regulator, educating the body to consume food only as needed.
Fasting saves time spent marketing, preparing and eating.
Fasting rids the body of toxins, giving it an "internal shower" & cleansing.
Fasting does not deprive the body of essential nutrients.
Fasting can be used to uncover the sources of food allergies.
Fasting is used effectively in schizophrenia treatment & other mental illnesses.
Fasting under proper supervision can be tolerated easily up to 4 weeks.
Fasting does not accumulate appetite; hunger "pangs" disappear in 1-2 days.
Fasting is routine for the animal kingdom.
Fasting has been a commonplace experience since man's existence.
Fasting is a rite in all religions; the Bible alone has 74 references to it.
Fasting under proper conditions is absolutely safe.
Fasting is not starving, it's nature's cure that God has given us. – Patricia Bragg
 – Allan Cott, M.D. *Fasting As A Way Of Life*

Spiritual Bible Reasons Why We Should Fast For A Healthier, Happier, Longer Walk with our Creator

3 John 2	Deut. 11:7-15, 21	Luke 9:11	Matthew 9:9-15
Gen. 6:3	Gal. 5:13-26	Mark 2:16-20	Neh. 9:1, 20-24
I Cor. 7:5	Isaiah 58	Matthew 4:1-4	Psalms 35:13
II Cor. 6	James 5:10-20	Matthew 6:6-18	Romans 16:16-20
Deut. 8:3	John 15	Matthew 7	Zechariah 8:19

Dear HEALTH FRIEND,

This is a gentle reminder of the great benefits from *The Miracle of Fasting* that you will enjoy once you get started on your weekly 24 hour Bragg Fasting Program for Super Health! It's a precious time of body-mind-soul cleansing and renewal.

On *fast* days I drink daily 7 to 9 glasses of pure distilled water or you can have some herb teas or diluted fresh juices. You may add 1 tablespoon of this mixture (1/2 oat bran and 1/2 psyllium husk powder) to these liquids twice a day and soak one minute before drinking! It's an extra cleanser and helps normalize weight, cholesterol, and blood pressures and helps maintain healthy elimination. Fasting is the oldest, most effective healing method known to man. Fasting offers many great and miraculous blessings from Mother Nature and our Creator. Fasting begins the self cleansing of the workings of the inner body so we can promote our own self-healing.

My father & I wrote the book *The Miracle of Fasting* to share with you the health miracles it can perform in your daily life and it's all so easy to do – it's an important part of the Bragg Healthy Lifestyle.   With Love,

Patricia Bragg

Paul Bragg's work on fasting is one of the great contributions to healing wisdom and the Natural Health Movement in the world today. – Gabriel Cousens, M.D., Author *Conscious Eating and Spiritual Nutrition.*

RIDDING THE BODY OF DANGEROUS
TOXIC WASTES BY CELL PURIFYING

Toxic poisons are the cause of most troubles in the human body. Most people do not have the vital force to supply the eliminative organs with the strength to move normal waste from the body. Without this vital energy the wastes are not flushed from the body. There they remain and lodge in the joints and organs of the body. We have a name for each symptom that gives us pain and trouble. Certain toxic wastes that are harmful to the whole body are rendered harmless by a substance in apple cider vinegar. Scientists call this protective action *Acetolysis*. Waste products broken down by this process are made harmless.

When you feel badly and do not seem to have the *Go Power* to do the things in life that are necessary – it is time to flush out the toxic wastes that your organs of elimination cannot seem to push out.

Remember your important organs of elimination are the bowel, the lungs, the skin and the kidneys. They are your faithful servants. They work hard 24 hours daily flushing out toxic wastes. Many times these eliminative organs must have help and that is when apple cider vinegar comes to their aid.

APPLE CIDER VINEGAR BODY PURIFICATION

Add 1 teaspoon ACV to six ounces of tomato or fresh vegetable juice (carrot and greens), and drink between meals, once or twice daily. Be sure to fast one day weekly and be faithful following the Bragg Healthy Lifestyle on page 28.

APPLE CIDER VINEGAR RELIEVES HEADACHES

People blame their headaches on many different organs of the body. Most headaches are blamed on the eyes, the nerves, the liver, the sinuses, the stomach, the bowels and kidneys. Headaches can be put in two classifications.

One type of chronic headache can be associated with long standing disease. The headache is a messenger telling the person that deep down in their body, destruction is going on and something should be done. This is Nature's great warning signal! There may be trouble in the liver, gallbladder, kidneys, bowel or in fact in any one of the important organs of the body to sinus-mucus problems, also allergies, etc.

The second type of headache is emotional. This is often caused by nervousness, anxiety, stress, strain, tension or any personal or emotional upsets.

This is a world where we must be associated with other human beings. Our daily life with others can throw us into upsetting emotional stress because they arouse in our being the emotions of fear, jealousy, envy, hate, greed, self-pity or self-indulgence. When emotions reach a boiling point you usually end up with a dull, aching headache. The worst type of headache is the migraine, which causes the sufferer to feel as if the head is splitting apart.

We have found in our many years of research on all kinds of headaches that when the body triggers a headache the urine is alkaline rather than its normal acid. It means the kidneys are disturbed by the emotions. It means that the body is off-balance. The malic acid of ACV can relieve headaches by aiding the kidneys to return to normal urine production.

Use of vaporized ACV can relieve headaches. In a small pan put 2 tablespoons of ACV and 1 cup distilled water. Bring mixture to boil. When fumes begin to rise, turn heat off, put a towel over your head and lean forward over fumes, taking ten deep breaths of the ACV and water mixture. Many sufferers of chronic headaches have told us they get blessed relief in 35 to 40 minutes with this method. In fact, they have said that after following the Bragg Healthy Lifestyle along with the ACV vapor method, they had no need for commercial headache and pain killers.

APPLE CIDER VINEGAR FOR COMBATING CORNS, CALLOUSES AND WARTS

For corns and callouses: First soak affected areas in warm water with 1/2 cup ACV for 20 to 30 minutes. After soaking, rub areas briskly with coarse towel, then gently use a pumice stone. Now apply a full strength ACV soaked gauze bandage overnight, and in the morning prepare a fresh ACV soaked bandage for daytime use. These treatments help soften and dissolve corns and callouses. Check your shoes, they are the biggest cause of irritating corns, callouses, bunions and blisters.

16

Give yourself weekly pedicures, and daily massage and exercise your feet, ideal while watching TV. Treat yourself to a foot reflexology or zone therapy treatment, see page 55. Be good to your feet – they are carrying you through life!

For Common Warts: Use the ACV treatment, *but caution: do not rub warts as this could spread them!* After soaking, use ACV soaked gauze bandage, keep on overnight. In the morning, for daytime treatment, apply a castor oil soaked gauze bandage. At night you can alternate ACV with crushed fresh garlic and vitamin E (cut open capsule). Combination treatments work wonders. If warts become a problem, some doctors freeze them with liquid nitrogen. This is fast, easy and leaves no scars.

FOR SUNBURNS

Lightly pat the skin with ACV to relieve sting and burning, and leave it on. This will give prompt relief. For all-over sunburns, pour one to two cups of ACV in cool bath water, then enjoy the healing, soothing soak. After soak pat on straight ACV to needed areas, then pat on aloe vera gel and leave on overnight. For serious burns, consult your doctor.

COMBATING SORE THROAT AND LARYNGITIS WITH APPLE CIDER VINEGAR

Apple cider vinegar is a dangerous enemy to all kinds of germs that attack the throat. To fight throat germs, ACV gargle mixture works miracles (1 tbsp to 1/2 glass of water). Do not use hot water, as it kills the enzymes. Three mouthfuls of the mixture is gargled each hour, and then spit out. Do not swallow the gargled mixture, because ACV acts like a sponge, drawing out throat germs and toxins from surrounding tissues. As the throat begins to feel better, extend gargling to once every three hours.

Along with the gargling, we use an ACV compress as follows: first, place a thin ACV soaked cloth over throat area, then place a hot, moist wrung-out towel to heat the throat and neck area, allowing ACV to absorb through the skin.

Even in good health, use ACV gargle once or twice weekly to help remove the body toxins being eliminated through the throat tissues. The gargle is also helpful during fasting, when the throat may produce a dark, stringy mucus as part of the detoxifying and cleansing process!

APPLE CIDER VINEGAR FOR
KEEPING THE SKIN HEALTHY

Reap vitality with the vinegar massage: In a small basin of warm water add one half cup of ACV. Dip both hands in the mixture and massage this all over the nude body (in shower or bathtub) – neck, chest, arms, shoulders, back, abdomen, legs, feet and face. Rub the mixture into the skin thoroughly. Be vigorous in your massage, but gentle on the face. Healthy skin has an acid reaction for it is throwing off toxic poisons through its billions of pores.

After thoroughly wetting the skin with the mixture several times, rub and massage until the skin is dry. Do this at least twice a week and do not wash it off; leave it on the body. As you massage the mixture in the skin you will feel a new vitality coming into your body.

The reason this treatment is far better than using soap is because soap has an alkaline reaction on the skin and this is just what you do not want! By keeping the skin in an acid reaction, your healthy skin will contribute to a healthy body.

We find after hard exercise or long mental work that we get a new feeling of strength and energy after one of these ACV massages. The next time you feel mentally or physically tired and worn-out, try this pep-building routine with ACV and water. We assure you, you will want to do it many, many times. The benefits will speak for themselves!

FOR SKIN BLEMISHES AND ACNE

To loosen dirt and grease from the face, turn off heat under a pan of steaming ACV water (3 tablespoons apple cider vinegar to quart of water). Put your face over the pan and use a towel draped over the head to trap the steam. Then pat ACV on the skin with a cotton ball to remove the loosened dirt. Repeat steaming and cleansing twice, then pat on chilled ACV, diluted with an equal amount of distilled water (store mix in refrigerator), to close pores and tone skin. Do steam cleansing 1 to 2 times weekly, as needed. Another excellent skin cleanser and toner is aloe gel or fresh aloe vera cactus pulp. Cut off 1 to 2 inches of aloe vera rib, slit open and rub directly on the skin.

YOUNGER LOOKING SKIN IN FIVE MINUTES WITH APPLE CIDER VINEGAR FACIAL

The skin consists of microscopically small flat scales that are constantly flaking off, thereby revealing the new skin beneath the outer, older layer of scales. In millions of people, the old, dead, dry outer scales do not peel off promptly, leaving thir skin old looking, dry, sallow, dull and lifeless for others to see. This is called the *old age look*.

Use this ACV facial for sensational results. First wash the skin in hot water (no soap). Next apply to the skin for three minutes a wrung-out, hot water-soaked towel. Remove. Soak a thin towel in warm water (containing 2 tbsp ACV per cup water), and apply to skin. Cover the ACV soaked towel with heavier towel wrung out in very hot water. Relax, lie down with feet elevated for 5 to 10 minutes.

Remove both towels, then rub skin gently with a coarse towel or loofah face pad. This last rub is to remove the millions of old, dry skin scales that have been detached and loosened by the ACV facial. You can repeat this weekly, as needed. Your skin will look fresh and youthful. The skin will shine with joyous new life. We all have a certain pride in looking our best and presenting a good personal appearance.

APPLE CIDER VINEGAR FOR ITCHING SCALP, DRY HAIR, DANDRUFF, THINNING HAIR AND BALDNESS

The high acidity (organic malic acid) plus the powerful enzymes (life chemicals) in ACV kill the *bottle bacillus*, a germ responsible for many scalp and hair conditions. The problems caused by bottle bacillus include itching scalp, dandruff, thinning hair and often baldness.*

Every hair has its own *oil can*. Bottle bacilli clogs the openings. Scales and small dry crusts are formed. Itching and dandruff result. The oil-starved hairs either fall out or break off, causing thinning of the hair and often baldness.

Apple cider vinegar not only kills bottle bacillus, but stimulates the oil cans to healthier, balanced activity.

Pour two tablespoons ACV in cup. Moisten cotton with water, then soak in the ACV. Part the hair in sections, and

* *Bragg Hair Book* gives a complete Hair Care Program. See back pgs for info.

apply directly to scalp. Leave on for at least fifteen minutes, up to two or three hours, before shampooing . . . this helps to restore the proper acid/alkaline balance to scalp. For acute cases, this should be done daily or before every shampoo.

For a healthy, after-shampoo rinse (also for body) add 1/3 cup apple cider vinegar to quart of rinse water.

HOW TO STRENGTHEN THE HEART

Take a little nip of ACV (2-3 drops) in 1/2 glass of distilled water, three times daily between meals. It's good especially before you take a walk or run or begin any exercise.

The heart is a large muscle and your master pump. It uses large amounts of potassium to keep going strong hour after hour for your entire life. It is the hardest working muscle in the body. It must have a constant and continuous supply of power and energy to continue beating. ACV contains a natural chemical that combines with heart fuel to make the heart muscle stronger. It also strengthens other muscles.

LOW-FAT MEALS CUT HEART DISEASE RISK

A 1993 British research report by Dr. George Miller of Britain's Medical Research Council stated, *High-fat meals make the blood more prone to clot within 6 to 7 hours after eating. Low-fat meals can almost immediately reverse this condition. Most heart attacks occur in the early morning, one reason may be the overnight clotting effects of a high-fat dinner. Researchers feel that by cutting fats from your diet, you may be able to add years to your life and cut the risk of heart disease!* These findings were supported by research at the University of Chicago. Safest is a low-fat, vegetarian diet.

FOR MUSCLE SORENESS AND ACHING JOINTS

To soothe tired aching muscles and joints, there is nothing like an ACV bath combined with a self-massage. While soaking in a warm bath to which one to two cups ACV have been added, slowly massage entire body, starting with soles of the feet. Gently but firmly squeeze and relax each part of the foot, working slowly up the right leg to hip, then repeat on left foot and leg. Continue up torso, then arms and neck, always rubbing towards heart. For face: lightly stroke skin in upward direction and avoid pulling facial skin down. Finish with fingertip massage in circular motions over scalp & head.

HOW TO IMPROVE DIGESTION

Millions have poor digestion (indigestion) aggravated by weak digestive and saliva juices, causing stomach distress: gas, heartburn and stomach bloating. *Five minutes before* mealtime, take tbsp distilled water with 1/3 tsp ACV. Before swallowing, hold in mouth for a few seconds. This draws saliva which starts to digest food right in the mouth. Before a meal, the diluted ACV causes stomach digestive fluids to flow faster and better, resulting in improved digestion. Never chew gum – especially on an empty stomach – because gum chewing fools the body and causes digestive juices to flow. This can cause ulcers, stomach problems, gas. etc.

FIGHT KIDNEY AND BLADDER PROBLEMS

Avoid animal, dairy, sugar, alcohol and caffeine products. All ages should follow the Bragg Healthy Lifestyle on page 28 for health and total body maintenance. Use ACV over salads and have your ACV cocktail in am, pm, etc.

ACV can help dissolve some types of kidney stones. Drink 8 to 10 glasses of pure liquids – especially organic cranberry juice which acidifies urine, inhibiting bacterial growth. Add 1/3 tsp ACV to each glass. If desired, sweeten with organic grape juice or honey. Also, do a three day watermelon (only) flush, chew seeds too; it's a great kidney-bladder cleanser.

For bedwetting: mix 1/2 to 1 tsp buckwheat honey with 1/3 tsp ACV before bedtime. Drink 7 to 8 glasses of pure distilled water daily. This is important for a healthy body, which is 65% water. Stop liquids three hours before bedtime.

For all kidney and bladder problems, drink healing and cleansing cornsilk (2 tbsp to quart water) or marshmallow tea, 2 to 3 times daily. Add 1/2 tsp ACV to each cup and sweeten with 1 tsp buckwheat honey. (Use fresh or dried corn silks and store in air-tight bottle.) I save corn silks for tea.

To soothe and heal bladder infections, add 1 cup ACV to warm sitz bath. Use 1 to 2 times daily. Use Dipstick tester from drugstore to check for any urinary infection.*

To keep bladder and sphincter muscle tightened and toned, urinate-stop-urinate-stop 5 to 6 times, twice daily when voiding. This helps you from getting the dribbles.

* Important: We don't endorse antibiotics, but if you are ever on them, please take acidophilus to replace the friendly bacteria.

COMBATING GALLSTONES WITH CIDER VINEGAR

Before starting the 2 day gallbladder flush, prepare for 1 week by drinking slowly upon arising, at mid-morning, mid-afternoon and after dinner: a 6 oz. glass apple juice with 1/3 tsp ACV, or dilute with distilled water if hypoglycemic. Apple juice is rich in malic acid, potassium, pectins and enzymes that act as solvents to soften and help remove debris (small stones & slush) and cleanse the body. Doctors have new methods for removing large stones.

No food is eaten during the next 2 day gallbladder flush.

Fill an 8 ounce glass with one part virgin olive oil (no substitutes) and two parts apple juice (organic is best), and add 1 tsp ACV. Take this mixture 3 times the first day. On the second day, take the mixture twice – on both days you may drink all the apple juice you desire – but no other liquid – not even water. This is not recommended for diabetics.

Sleep on right side when on flush, pulling
right knee toward chest to open pathway.

About midmorning of the 3rd day eat a raw (nature's broom) variety salad – of cabbage, carrots, celery, beet, tomatoes, sprouts and lettuce with generous amounts of ACV and olive oil. If desired, have a bowl of lightly steamed greens such as spinach, kale, collards, chard or other leafy greens.

This miracle cleanser flush I take once a year. Check your bowel movements for tiny greenish-brown stones. It is amazing what your gallbladder, stomach & colon will flush!

Note: Mild nausea may occur. This shows toxins, mucus and bile are being dumped in the stomach, and your body wants it out! If nauseated, your body is telling you: drink 1 to 2 glasses distilled water and regurgitate. Once it's out, you feel better right away!

CIDER VINEGAR HELPS SHRINK PROSTATE GLAND

With a fork "whip" 2 tbsp ACV with 2 tbsp olive oil, a dash of cinnamon and Bragg Liquid Aminos. Use this ACV mixture daily over salads, sliced tomatoes, avocados and steamed veggies. Remember to take a Zinc supplement (80 mg. daily) for the prostate. Raw pumpkin seeds are rich in Zinc.

CIDER VINEGAR FOR FEMALE TROUBLES

For a healthier vagina, use ACV douches when needed as the acidity is approximately the same as the vagina.

Douche mixture: 3 tablespoons ACV to 2 quarts warm distilled water is a cleansing, healing douche. If discharge, use 1 to 2 times daily, less frequently as discharge lessens.

To shrink, tighten and tone a flabby womb, eat raw garden salads made with extra parsley and celery, on which 1 teaspoon of apple cider vinegar is sprinkled. Olive, soy, sunflower, safflower & canola oils are unsaturated, and may be added for flavor along with a dash of Bragg Liquid Aminos.

HOW TO FIGHT ARTHRITIS WITH CIDER VINEGAR

Hard stony deposits fill up and cement the joints. Some stony deposits enlarge and cripple the joints. Crippling, painful arthritis and joint problems are the sad results!

Fight and help flush out those stony deposits with ACV and the Bragg Healthy Lifestyle. Eat 65-75% healthy raw foods – organic is best, and drink distilled water (chemical and inorganic mineral free), and take your vitamin and mineral supplements, kelp and alfalfa tablets and 1 teaspoon cod liver oil daily – and you will see great improvements!

Upon arising have your delicious ACV cocktail as follows: stir, shake or blend 6 oz. distilled water with 1 to 2 tsp ACV and 1 to 2 tsp honey. Follow this by eating an organic apple. Use 1 teaspoon ACV with your daily garden salad and remember . . . *1 to 2 apples a day help keep the doctor away.*

CIDER VINEGAR COMBATS MUCUS CONDITIONS

Millions are plagued with mucus from the sinus cavities, nose and throat, and have post-nasal drip, which are all most uncomfortable. If the mucus sufferer will discontinue all dairy products, eggs and sugars from their diet, and follow the Bragg Healthy Lifestyle with a weekly 24 hour fast (see pg 14) and use plenty of ACV, these mucus conditions vanish.

Upon arising have glass of warm distilled water with 1 tsp honey and 1 to 2 tsp ACV. Also enjoy this drink mid-morning and afternoon. On your daily salads use 1 to 2 tsp ACV combined with olive oil and dash or spray of Bragg Liquid Aminos. Put Bragg Aminos in spray bottle – great method for seasoning salads, popcorn, etc. – and take when dining out.

It is also helpful to use ACV throat gargles and nasal sniff washes (1 to 2 tsp ACV to glass warm water) twice daily until mucus conditions leave. Along with ACV cocktail, fresh carrot & green juices can be enjoyed between meals. The important thing is to sip your juices very slowly, as they are really foods, not beverages. A small amount in the mouth at one time will be better digested & more easily used by the body chemistry.

FOR NOSEBLEEDS

Soak cotton ball or gauze in ACV and lightly pack in nostrils. Press nostrils together 3 to 5 minutes, while vinegar helps blood congeal. Vitamins C and K are also helpful.

CIDER VINEGAR AND CONSTIPATION

It is important that the bowels move regularly and freely. Out-go should equal in-take. You should have a bowel movement upon arising and one within an hour after each meal. Flaxseed tea with ACV acts as a bowel lubricant.

How to make an ACV bowel lubricant drink: boil two cups distilled water and add 2 tablespoons flaxseed. Continue to boil for ten minutes. Strain off flaxseed, the liquid becomes jelly-like. If needed, dilute with more water before drinking. Upon arising daily drink a cup of it with 1 teaspoon ACV until you get good daily bowel movements.

Another super bowel cleanser to use: add 1 tablespoon (1/2 oat bran and 1/2 psyllium husk powder) to the ACV cocktail, a glass distilled water, herb tea, diluted juice or the ACV-flaxseed lubricant drink; let soak one minute before drinking!

For easier flowing bowel movements: elevate feet 6 to 10 inches in front of toilet, then from behind use your second and third fingers to gently pull up on the edge of the anus.

To check elimination time: have some fresh or frozen whole corn with your evening meal. Purposely do not chew all kernels, check stools to see when they are eliminated, should be within 10 to 14 hours. When the body is cleansed of toxins and malnutrition ("mal" means bad), the body becomes healthier and starts working more normally.

Because constipation brings on many health problems, including arthritis, it is important to cleanse & open your pipes (colon & arteries) by following the Bragg Healthy Lifestyle.

I do not generally recommend enemas or colonics except in emergency situations or fasts. Excessive colonic use especially weakens peristalsis activity and can drain your body energy. But a 12 minute retention enema can help loosen debris being purged from colon walls during a fast.
– Gabriel Cousens M.D., author of Conscious Eating

The body is self-healing and self-repairing. It is our duty if we want vibrant, glorious health to do all we can to make the body work efficiently to maintain vital, super health.

Not only is a healthy diet necessary, but also needed are good sleeping habits, outdoor physical activity, full deep breathing and a serene mind. Man cannot live by bread alone. Man must have spiritual food. Man must strive for a perfect healthy balance: physical, mental, emotional and spiritual!

WHAT BECOMES OF THE ACID CRYSTALS PRECIPITATED IN THE BODY

You have often heard the expression . . . *He's old and stiff and his flesh is tough.* When we think of *old* people we think of them as stiff in the moving joints of the body and that their flesh is tough and brittle. (See Dr. Carrel page 7)

Why do people get stiff in the joints and their flesh get tough when they have added birthdays to their life? Most people would answer this complex question with the remark, *because they are old.* But this is not the answer to why people get stiff joints and tough flesh. The answer to premature ageing is unhealthy living and a potassium deficiency. People rarely study their bodies, or learn to eat for healthy tissues and joint youthfulness. They are satisfied to eat *what agrees with them* and let it go at that. Or they eat foods they were reared on as children and carry these early eating habits, (often un-healthy) right into their adult life and then into their children's lives! *Ignorance in action destroys health.*

REARING HEALTHY CHILDREN

The Bragg family children, grandchildren and great-grandchildren, etc. have all been reared on the Bragg Healthy Lifestyle. We were taught to keep in perfect health, so that the body tissues would remain soft, tender and have elasticity and health. This correct way of eating enables them to come to the later years of life with youthful-looking skin, keen hearing, sharp sparkling eyes and perfect mental, emotional and physical health, for a long and healthy life.

You are what you eat, drink, breathe, think and do!   – Patricia Bragg

MIRACLES WITH APPLE CIDER VINEGAR

The Bragg family follow the Bragg Healthy Lifestyle. They have learned the lessons of good nutrition and the miracles of ACV for themselves and their animals. The children were impressed when Farmer Bragg would have an old hen prepared for dinner. The old hen's meat was tough and didn't taste good. This is what happens to poultry and beef when it is deficient in potassium. Human flesh suffers the same problems.

To prove to the children conclusively that apple cider vinegar and honey needed to be an important part of their daily nutrition he would then select another old hen for the dinner table. This time he fed that old hen ACV twice a day. For a week to ten days he gave the hen the ACV mixture. When the hen was prepared for the dinner table, the children saw the difference in the old hen's meat. They saw how tender it was. It was just like eating a young hen. It was so delicious, they asked for second helpings. *Most of the Bragg Family are now happy, healthy vegetarians.*

ALL YOUR LIFE
YOU MUST FIGHT ACID CRYSTALS,
THEY CAUSE PREMATURE AGEING

When acid crystals harden in the joints and tissues of any animal, the joints become stiff and the tissues hardened. The meat becomes tough and tasteless. But when the animals are given apple cider vinegar regularly, the precipitated acid crystals enter into a solution and pass out of the body, thus making the body tissues healthier and tender. This applies to human flesh also.

Now when body tissues hold all the precipitated acid crystals they can, the crystals then appear in the bursae and the joints of the body resulting in arthritis and bursitis. 1 to 2 tsp of apple cider vinegar with 1 to 2 tsp of raw honey in a glass of distilled water daily will help relieve the stiff aching and prematurely old joints . You be the judge. See how elastic and well oiled your joints will become.

KEEP JOINTS AND TISSUES YOUTHFUL

Most people have lost their normal contact with nature and simple natural living. They no longer know how to eat the way God intended.

If you suffer from premature old joints and hardened tissues take the ACV mixture several times daily. Eliminate or cut down on animal proteins and stop all refined sugars and see how very youthful your body will feel.

You will find after several months of the ACV and honey cocktail taken once or twice daily, the misery will be gone from your joints. You will discover you can walk or run up several flights of stairs without any effort. You will notice that you look younger and above all, that you feel younger than you have for years.

Make the Bragg Healthy Lifestyle (pg 28) a daily habit. Over the years we have seen many stiff-jointed, prematurely old people, transform themselves into new, youthful, healthy people. We cannot do it for you. You must make the effort to give this ACV and honey program a chance to prove what it can do for you! We challenge you to begin today!

QUESTIONS ASKED ABOUT
APPLE CIDER VINEGAR

Many people have some preconceived idea that natural apple cider vinegar is harmful to the body. It is distilled, malt and synthetic vinegars that must be avoided.

Let us assure you that there is nothing in this wonderful natural apple cider vinegar that can in any way harm your body! People ask us about the merits and benefits of apple cider vinegar. See the inside front cover for some of the miracles of apple cider vinegar.

Animal proteins and fats have a tendency to thicken the blood and the natural acids in apple cider vinegar help to keep the blood healthier and thinner.

People naturally crave and serve cranberry sauce (which contains four different natural acids) with turkey and other fowl. They serve apple sauce with roast pork dishes. Or a slice of lemon with fish. Or steak with mushrooms, which are rich in citric acid also.

Natural food acids served along with animal proteins are designed to lessen the thickening influence of these heavy proteins. In order for blood to circulate freely throughout the body, the blood should be thin. When blood thickens, it puts a strain on the heart. Then the blood pressure goes up and other problems start.

Remember blood has to circulate all over the body through the arteries, blood vessels and tiny capillaries. It is impossible for blood to circulate freely through these hair-like pipes when it is thickened with too much protein.

Several years ago we met a woman with extremely high blood pressure. We put her on a two day ACV, honey and water program with nothing to eat for 48 hours. She had an ACV cocktail 5 times daily, plus 4 glasses of distilled water.

In forty-eight hours her blood pressure had dropped many points. The buzzing in the ears ceased, and her dull headache stopped. In a short period of correct eating (no salt, saturated fats, tea, coffee, etc.) combined with her daily ACV program she brought her blood pressure back to normal.

People ask us if apple cider vinegar dries up the blood. If apple cider vinegar will make them thin and skinny. We have been using the apple cider vinegar program in the Bragg family for over five generations and it has done wonderful things for our health and bodies.

THE BRAGG HEALTHY LIFESTYLE PROMOTES VITAL SUPER HEALTH

Bragg Healthy Lifestyle consists of eating 65 to 75% of your diet from fresh organic live foods, raw vegetables, salads, sprouts, fresh fruits and fresh juices, raw seeds and nuts, 100% whole-grain breads, pastas and cereals and the nutritious beans and legumes – these are the no-cholesterol, no-fat, no-salt, just simple *live foods* body fuel for more health that make live people. This is the reason people become revitalized and reborn into a fresh new life filled with Joy, Health, Vitality, Youthfulness and Longevity! There are millions of Bragg Healthy Lifestyle followers around the world proving this works!

FIVE GENERATIONS OF HEALTHY BRAGGS –
ALL USING APPLE CIDER VINEGAR

Since birth all the Bragg children have used apple cider vinegar. They fed it to their children, and now grandchildren are feeding it to great grandchildren. We all use ACV and unsaturated oil (olive, soy, canola and safflower oils) on our salads. We put it on our steamed greens (spinach, kale, mustard greens, chard, beet tops), and many other foods.

Millions of our students around the world have used it, and never once has anyone reported a negative reaction from using it. In fact, they sing its praises. So you can only benefit from using the ACV, honey and water program.

APPLE CIDER VINEGAR AND ARTHRITIS

People ask if AVC will cure their arthritis. This is not possible. Curing is an internal biological function that only the body can do.

A scientific natural diet, deep breathing, exercise, rest, relaxation, and all forms of natural hygiene are required to put the body in a condition to *Cure Itself.* Apple cider vinegar is an important part of the program. When all of the supreme forces of nature are used, the body will turn from the sick side to the well side. Health is something you must desire, earn and always be strong and protect!

Jesus said: *Thy faith hath made thee whole, and go and sin no more.* And that means your dietetic sins. He himself, through fasting and prayer, was able to heal the sick and cure all manner of diseases.

Fixing Life's Flats: *When your life seems a bit flat, look around for a source of leakage! Life habits, actions, words, deeds, thoughts – are they healthy and happy? Just a little leak in time will cause a tire to go flat and your life too! Check your life for leaks – and stop them now!* – Patricia Bragg

29

FIGHTING MUSCLE CRAMPS
WITH APPLE CIDER VINEGAR

Many people are awakened in the middle of the night with sharp, painful muscle cramps. These often appear in the feet and lower or upper legs. Sometimes they appear in the stomach, intestines and occasionally in the heart. These are frightening experiences! Most people who experience cramps in the legs are forced to jump out of bed and pound the cramped leg to get relief. Many people with cramps in other parts of the body have to walk quickly to get relief.

When precipitated acid crystals get into the circulation of the legs and other parts of the body they can cause severe cramps. We recommend taking two teaspoons ACV and tone teaspoon of honey in a glass of distilled water three times daily to relieve these painful cramps. This allows the precipitated acid crystals to enter into a solution and pass out of the body, causing the painful cramps to cease.

YOU MUST FIGHT ACID CRYSTALS
THEY CAUSE PREMATURE AGEING

The healthiest person in the world must continually fight the buildup of acid crystals in the body. The strongest enemy of acid crystals is the apple cider vinegar, honey and water cocktail. This powerful mixture puts the acid crystals in solution so they can be flushed out of the body by the kidneys and other organs of elimination.

MAKE THIS 48 HOUR TEST

For two full days take nothing into your system but liquids. Have the apple cider vinegar, honey and water cocktail 3 to 5 times daily. Be sure to drink 4 to 5 glasses of distilled water daily as well.

On the second and third day after you have eaten nothing else for 48 hours, take a sample of your first early morning urine. Put these urine samples in bottles with lids. Place them on a shelf and let it stand. After two weeks examine them in the sunlight. You will see with your own eyes the sediment on the bottom of the bottles. These are the disease-causing toxins that have been flushed out of your body!

POTASSIUM — THE MASTER MINERAL

Always keep the fact in mind that potassium puts toxic poisons in solution so they can be flushed out of the body. The body is self-healing and self-repairing. Just give it the tools to work with and you will have a painless, tireless, ageless body, regardless of your age! Forget age and calendar years . . . for age is not toxic! You age prematurely because you suffer from nutritional deficiencies and because of the fact your Vital Force is low and you have poor body drainage.

The Bragg Healthy Lifestyle will help you rebuild your Vital Force. Watch the transformation that will take place in your body when you faithfully follow your ACV regime. You will and can create the kind of person you want to be!

Although you must follow this program closely, do not try to do everything listed here immediately. Remember it took you a long time and wrong habits of living to cause any of the problems your body might have now. So, it's going to take time for the body to rebuild and repair itself into a more *perfect health home* for you! Please remember your body is your *temple* while on this earth – so cherish and protect it!

My father and I have shared the Bragg Healthy Lifestyle Blueprint with millions of people around the world at the Bragg Health and Fitness Crusades. I would now like to share it it with you as it's part of the Apple Cider Vinegar Health System.

With Blessings of Health, Peace, Joy and Love,

I cannot overstate the importance of the habit of quiet meditation and prayer for more health of body, mind and spirit – *In quietness . . . shall be your strength.*   – Isaiah 30:15

WE THANK THEE

For flowers that bloom about our feet;
For song of bird and hum of bee;
For all things fair we hear or see,
Father in heaven we thank Thee!
For blue of stream and blue of sky;
For pleasant shade of branches high;
For fragrant air and cooling breeze;
For beauty of the blooming trees
Father in heaven we thank Thee!
For mother love and fathercare,
For brothers strong and sisters fair;
For love at home and here each day;
For guidance lest we go astray,
Father in heaven we thank Thee!
For this new morning with its light;
For rest and shelter of the night;
For health and food, for love and friends;
For every thing His goodness sends
Father in heaven we thank Thee!
- Ralph Waldo Emerson

Jack LaLanne, Patricia Bragg, Elaine LaLanne & Paul C. Bragg

Jack says, "Bragg saved my life at age 15 when I attended the Bragg Health and Fitness Crusade in Oakland, California." From that day on he has continued to live a healthy lifestyle, inspiring millions to Health and Fitness.

BRAGG HEALTHY LIFESTYLE

🌸🌸🌸🌸🌸🌸🌸🌸

The Bragg Blueprint for Physical, Mental and Spiritual Improvement – Healthy, Vital Living to 120

By

Patricia Bragg, N.D., Ph.D.

Life Extension Nutritionist

Just think: in 90 days you can build a new bloodstream! Not a thick, sluggish, toxic-saturated bloodstream, but a rich red bloodstream healthy in all the vitamins, minerals and vital nutrients necessary for radiant and long lasting health. First and foremost, we must build the iron content of our bloodstream. This is one of the great secrets of life: the more iron in your bloodstream, the more *oxygen* is going to flood into your body, purifying every one of the cells of your body. Oxygen is the greatest stimulant in the world. It stimulates, but does not depress. Unnatural stimulants stimulate, but there is an aftermath of depression. Tobacco, alcohol, coffee, tea, refined white sugar and drugs (prescribed and over-the-counter) have this effect on the body, but not God's own oxygen! It is the invisible staff of life!

So, in the Bragg Healthy Lifestyle we forever discard these harmful destroying stimulants. These are never going to enter your body! You are going to rely on the wonderful, natural stimulants to create a more Healthy Vital Force. First, you are going to follow the Bragg Deep Breathing Program that's so important to the Bragg Healthy Lifestyle. You are going to use live foods such as: fresh fruits & vegetables and freshly squeezed juices that help build your vital blood sugar.

Before you eat or drink anything – I want you to ask your self this important question, *Is this going to build a healthy bloodstream or help destroy it?* Be on the alert to protect your precious river of life – your bloodstream! When it demands liquids, give it pure water (distilled is best) or live

---

Man's days shall be to 120 years – Genesis 6:3

food juices such as fresh fruit and vegetable juices. Get yourself a juicer. Every day you can fortify your bloodstream with fresh orange, grapefruit, or carrot & greens – or combine different juices such as celery, tomato, beet & parsley. Two of the best juices to add with these vegetable juices are made from raw spinach and watercress. For a taste delight add the juice of 1 to 2 garlic buds. Garlic is an excellent purifier.

Do not consume too much of these powerful live food juices. 1 to 2 pints a day is more than enough. Some people get a juicer, and they go overboard. Overloading your body with juices can upset your delicate sugar balance.

Just because something is good for you, that does not mean that a lot of it is. As with all things in life, moderation in your food intake is best for building Vitality Supreme!

Imagine it: in just 11 months you will have an absolutely New You! The billions of soft cells that make up eyes, nose, skin, hands, feet, as well as all the vital organs of your body, will be renewed. You do not need to submit to the huge risk of a heart, kidney or any other dangerous transplant.

You have within your power, through the food you eat, the liquid you drink, and the air you breathe, to build a fresh vital body from the top of your head, to the tip of your toes. You are what you eat and what you eat today will be walking and talking tomorrow! How wonderful our Creator has been to us, to give us the power every 90 days to build a new bloodstream and every 11 months an entirely new body.

The Creator gave us the intelligence and reasoning power to control our healthy bodies. But the flesh is dumb! You can stuff anything in your stomach and almost get away with it!

Most young people live this way, because they believe they are totally indestructible. But what a sad, sad lesson they learn after 40 or 50 years of wrong living as the miseries and the aches and pains creep into their bodies: making life miserable & a lie of their myth & dream of indestructibility.

Who is strong? He who can conquer his bad habits. – Ben Franklin

Laws of health are inexorable; we see people going down and out in the prime of life simply because no attention is paid to them! – Paul C. Bragg

Live by the reasoning mind rather than by the senses of the body. The dumb senses are constantly enticing you to do the very things that destroy your wonderful body. Look around you – look at the horrible human sights you see. Weak people, mentally depressed people, and sickness everywhere. The average person's suffering is self-inflicted.

For whatsoever a man soweth, that shall he also reap. (Gal. 6:7) We should know and observe the fact that everything in the Universe is always governed by definite laws – with no exceptions. If we understand and follow these laws – we will sow the seeds of constructive healthy living!

Make Every Day a Healthy Day – and each day you will improve! You will feel the new strength and energy flooding into your body. The feeling you will experience when you live the true natural health life is indescribable. What an incredibly powerful and joyful feeling it is: to be fully alive, vigorous, with unlimited energy and powerful nerve force.

IT'S NEVER TOO LATE FOR YOU TO BUILD RADIANT HEALTH!

Weak people find weak excuses in order to continue their bad habits of living. They will tell you they are too old to begin the Bragg Healthy Lifestyle Program. Age has no force nor is it toxic. Time is just a measure, nothing more and nothing less. Long ago the Bragg Family gave up living in calendar years. We only live in biological years. There are millions in their 30's and 40's who are, I'm sad to state . . . prematurely old biologically. Yet there are many people in their 60's, 70's, 80's and 90's who are biologically young.

In my opinion, if you are experiencing premature ageing you are suffering from a highly toxic condition and you are suffering from unnecessary nutritional deficiencies. This is the main cause of most human troubles. Our program will show you how to banish these two vicious enemies.

Prayer is the mortar that holds our house together.
– Sister Teresa, James 5:16

Whatsoever was the father of a disease; an ill diet was the mother.
– Herbert, 1859

From this minute on, stop living by calendar years! Just forget your birthdays, as I do. All of us are reborn every second of the day as new body cells are being created.

Cease this talk of *getting old!* From this minute on, you will have no age except your biological age and this you are going to control. Every day say to yourself repeatedly, *I Will Never Grow Old!* Burn it deeply in your conscious mind and above all bury it deeply in your subconscious.

Most people have a dreadful fear of *getting old.* They picture themselves half-blind, hearing impaired, teeth gone, energy and vitality spent, senile. They see themselves a burden to their family and friends. They envision themselves in the old people's home: alone, forsaken and forgotten.

Despite the fear of old age and the train of ailments that go with *getting old,* you can prevent this human tragedy.

You can skip this terrible period by how you live from this day forward. Today is the day to prepare against senility and decrepitude. That is why I urge you to follow the wise and wonderful Laws of Mother Nature. You will grow younger as you live longer! That is what this program is all about: The Preservation of Your Vital Health!

PREVENTION KEEPS YOU
YOUNG, VITAL AND VIGOROUS!

Lengthening life by special treatment of chronic miseries often means merely adding years of ill-health and misery to a person's life – what is often called *the living death.* Who wants to extend life just to suffer? In my opinion, the true function of the Healer today is to prevent sickness & disease.

No man is able to heal you! Only you can heal yourself! In order to be healthy it is essential for you to know how to live in order to be well always. *An ounce of prevention is worth a pound of cure!*

Diet for Health and Youthfulness – Your diet should be composed of at least 65% raw fruit, and raw or properly cooked (steamed, baked or wokked) vegetables. By this habit such conditions as stomach upsets, miseries and constipation which occur so often in children and adults can be avoided! Out-go should equal intake. You should have a bowel movement upon arising and after each meal.

Our greatest enemy to health is constipation . . . and this can be eliminated by a diet that gives you sufficient bulk moisture, lubrication and vigorous exercise of the entire abdominal cavity. In the remote parts of the world where we have traveled beyond the influences of so-called modern civilization, mankind indulges in the normal habit of defecation after every meal. I want you to train yourself to have a bowel movement upon arising and after each meal. Children can be taught this habit from infancy. With the Bragg Healthy Lifestyle constipation vanishes.

Constipation Creates Toxins in the Body – Studies reveal the presence of toxic poison (toxins) in cases of constipation. When these toxins are absorbed into the general circulation, the liver, which is your detoxifying organ is unable to cope with them. These toxins then are thrown back in the body and cause trouble and sickness. *Toxemia is our real enemy!*

I firmly believe diet plays a very important role in the maintenance of health and the prevention of pathological conditions. I have found in my research that diets composed of refined white flour and sugar, preserved meats such as hot dogs and lunch meats, white rice, coffee, tea, cola drinks, alcohol, margarine, over-cooked vegetables, over-cooked meats and salted foods can bring on many miseries in the human body, especially miseries of the respiratory and the gastro-intestinal tracts. *None of these refined, processed, embalmed, dead unhealthy foods should be eaten by You!*

YOUR ENERGY IS YOUR BODY'S SPARK PLUG

Your Energy comes from the spark of life which is maintained by the atomic energy contained within every single cell of the human body. It embodies electrons, protons, neutrons, positrons and alpha particles. They are constantly discharging their ionic compounds as energy is expended in work – whether mental or physical – in accordance with Natural Laws. This energy loss must be replaced. Every cell in your body is like a battery which when run down must be recharged. Primarily this is done through the intake of food. Proper breathing and exercise also help recharge the cells.

Now there are two kinds of food. The first is in a low rate of physical vibration, such as the foods we have mentioned: the processed, chemicalized, *non-foods*, such as refined white flour and sugars, etc. It is *impossible* to have a youthful, dynamic body when year after year you feed it foods and drinks with a low rate of vibration.

The Bragg Healthy Lifestyle Program consist only of the second kind of foods: those in a high rate of vibration. Many people have the preconceived idea that protein is the food that is in the highest rate of vibration. While protein is an important nutrient to the human body, fresh fruit has a higher rate of vibration. Fruit produces blood sugar which helps to feed the nerves of the body. Fruit has a two-fold purpose in the body. First, it's rich in blood sugar; second, it's an important, needed detoxifier and destroyer of harmful obstructions, wastes, and toxins that can do great harm.

Often you will hear people say, *I am allergic to apples, grapefruit, peaches, strawberries, etc.!* These people have no idea what these foods are doing in their bodies. To give you an example, when my father Paul C. Bragg was reared in the South many years ago, his typical Southern diet was rich in animal proteins and fats from the hogs, chickens, beef, sheep and fowl they raised. At each meal they had a wide variety of these meat proteins. I'm sad to state that accompanying these were white flour biscuits and bread, mashed and fried potatoes and, inevitably, a heavy, sugary dessert.

When he ate strawberries, tomatoes, green peppers and many other fruits, he would break out in painful red itching hives. When he attended military school from 12 on, his body became so saturated with toxic poisons, mucus and putrid food residues that, when he ate any fresh fruits, he suffered not only hives, but also colds, headaches, aches and pains, etc. as well. These were erroneously thought to be allergic reactions, but they were the natural responses of a body that wanted to be healthy and clean. The cleansing fruits were helping to clean his body and push out the toxins!

He refrained from eating these vital foods until he became a health advocate at the age of sixteen.

Only after he had been cleansed and purified with healthy foods, apple cider vinegar and fasting one day a week, along with occasional longer fasts, could he eat fresh fruits and vegetables without a negative reaction. Through fasting and careful nutrition he slowly detoxified himself and could eat all the wonderful natural foods without experiencing the allergic cleansing reactions of his youth. His TB was the outcome of the wrong foods he ate.

For this the reason people who have been living on a diet high in animal proteins and fats, starches, refined sugars and saturated fats cannot immediately include a large amount of fresh fruits and raw vegetables into their diet. . . but it's best to flow into the Bragg Healthy Lifestyle and allow the body to gently start cleansing.

The Transition Diet – Everyone who wants to live the healthy life must thoroughly understand just what is going on in their body chemistry. Fresh raw fruit and fresh vegetables help flush toxins out of the body. But the body cannot be rushed. It takes the average person a long time to saturate the body with toxic poisons and, likewise it is going to take time for this debris to be flushed out!

The more organic raw fruits and raw vegetables that you have conditioned yourself to handle, the more cleansed your body will become! So, recognize these foods which are in the highest rate of healthy vibration. But please, also respect their great cleansing and detoxifying action!

We often eat 100 % raw fruits, vegetables, salads for a few days, but usually our meals are 60 to 70% raw:

BREAKFAST: Fresh raw juice (orange, grapefruit or carrot, celery, garlic, spinach, etc.) and later raw fruit (melon, apple, banana, etc.) or . . . the nutritious, delicious, and easy to prepare Bragg Pep Drink – see recipe on page 62.

LUNCH: Large raw combination salad with fresh greens, vegetables, sprouts and a few raw nuts or seeds (sunflower, sesame, pumpkin, almonds, pecans, walnuts, etc.)

DINNER: Variety salad, followed by two steamed, baked or wokked fresh vegetables and one of following: beans, lentils, brown rice, whole grain pasta, tofu, baked or steamed potatoes.

Remember to get your daily apple cider vinegar into your diet with the ACV Cocktail and sprinkle ACV over steamed greens, cauliflower, squash, broccoli, cabbage, stringbeans, etc. It is also especially delicious on garden variety salads.

People are told that they must start the day with a big breakfast as this will give great energy in the morning hours when they need energy badly. So, they heavily gorge themselves on processed cereal with cream and sugar; ham and eggs; or bacon and eggs; hot cakes or stacks of buttered toast and jelly. All this washed down with coffee, milk or cocoa. You will note there is no fruit at this meal.

Only a person doing the most strenuous physical labor could possibly burn up a meal like this. (And I doubt even that.) All the vital energy of the body will be needed to digest these heavy animal proteins and fats, refined starch, and white sugar breakfasts. All too often they lie on the stomach like a ton of bricks and have to be dynamited out. Now you know why there is so much indigestion and constipation and why laxatives are one of the biggest sellers in drug stores.

So, I ask you, how in the name of common sense can a big meal like this give a person strength for the morning duties? The truth of the matter is, it can't. This is how mothers, and consequently their children, are brain-washed by the big food interests who sell all their commercial *unhealthy foods.*

You Must Change Your Ideas About Food – Learn to eat in moderation. It is important that you not overfuel your body. If you overfeed your body you will clog it up. A diet rich in an abundance of healthy raw foods with a high rate of vibration will keep your insides clean and vitalized.

MIRACLE OF FASTING*
MASTER KEY TO INTERNAL PURIFICATION

If you will do a complete water fast for 24 hours each week, soon you will be able to add more fresh fruit and vegetables to your diet. After a fast of 3 to 7 days you can include even more foods that are in a high rate of vibration.

We faithfully fast 24 hours every Monday and the first 3 days of each month. Wait until you experience this. You will greatly benefit from the inner cleansing and will love the pure, clean feeling you receive! Read page 14.

* For important Fasting & Cleansing info read this mighty Bragg Book for Super Health: *The Miracle of Fasting.* See back pages for details.

FASTING BRINGS REMARKABLE RESULTS

Stated Professor A. E. Crews of Edinburgh University, who studied both worms and animals. *Given appropriate and essential conditions of the environment, including proper care of the body . . . Eternal Youth, in fact, can be a reality in living forms. It's found to be possible by repeated processes of fasting to keep a worm alive twenty times longer than it would have lived in the regular way. This has also been proven with animals.* Something to think about indeed.

Remember it took time for the body to build up toxins, so it takes time to unload them. Take your time. Be faithful to the Bragg Healthy Lifestyle Program. You will reap wonderful benefits. Cut down on all concentrated foods gradually.

Vegetables contain many excellent proteins: Soy beans, brown and wild rice, dried lima beans, garbanzos, split peas, lentils, pinto beans, kidney beans are excellent sources of protein. Remember: beans are a good source of protein and also magnesium, which is so necessary to your heart and for good nutritional health.

If you desire meat – *do not eat red meat more than 2 to 3 times a week.* Meat has uric acid, urea, saturated fats and cholesterol. These are all highly toxic materials and are not good for the body. Some days, in place of red meat, substitute fish, because it is a cleaner protein and a less saturated fat, or chicken or turkey which have significantly less uric acid, urea and saturated fat than red meat. Healthy, free range poultry is better for you than red meat.

Eggs should not be eaten over 4 times weekly. They are a highly concentrated food with cholesterol – a saturated fat – in the yolk. If your cholesterol count is over 200, it's best to leave eggs out of your diet until your cholesterol gets to 180 or lower. (Read page 59.) Cheeses, are also highly concentrated. If you eat cheese, be sure it is naturally aged – not processed cheese, and eat only sparingly. Dairy products are mucous producing and all milk products and eggs are best eaten sparingly or not at all!

If you have been eating an unbalanced breakfast, you need to begin including more fresh fruit and *slowly cut down* on the concentrated foods. If you have been eating bacon or ham, white breads, sweetrolls, etc., omit these processed, refined, preserved foods. They are foods with an extremely low rate of vibration. Instead of eating two eggs per day, eat only one and soon you can cut down to only four per week.

Stewed prunes, raw wheat germ and honey with fresh fruit make a nutritious breakfast. In time you can learn to eat lightly or not at all . . . most people don't need breakfast.

There were never two people any more physically and mentally active than my father and I. We never ate breakfast, other than fresh fruit. But before we ate even that, we did all our morning exercises, our deep breathing, or had a long hike or swim. Our day usually began around 5 am and we were busy until 10 am or later before we ate our fresh fruit. Many mornings we were so busy with writing books and our outdoor activities: organic gardening, hiking, swimming and tennis, that we did not even take time to eat.

I believe most people over-eat! That is the reason their vitality is at such a low ebb. Don't overeat – even if it is good health foods. Help your body detoxify by giving it cleansing time. When you eat, your body is forced to work on the digestion of this food and has no energy for detoxification. So the toxins pile up and you accumulate physical miseries and age prematurely. Don't kill yourself with overstuffing!

THE "SECRET" OF HEALTH
LIES IN INTERNAL CLEANLINESS

That is what you want to strive for – a toxicless body! Gradually include more fresh fruit and raw vegetables into your diet. Have fresh fruit in the morning and a large raw combination vegetable salad at noon and, if desired, some fresh fruit for dessert, if you like. Eat a yellow vegetable, such as yam, sweet potato, yellow squash or carrots, and a green vegetable every day. Cook these vegetables by baking, steaming or wokking them.

With your main meal you may have a more concentrated form of protein. Our favorite forms of protein are vegetarian. But, in moderation, animal proteins such as meat, fish, eggs, and natural cheese are okay. Your diet should include raw nuts and seeds (such as sunflower, pumpkin, sesame, etc.) and avocados. Enjoy beans, brown rice, and legumes 3 times a week. By having a variety of God's natural foods you will enjoy a balanced diet and a healthier balanced life.

You may use the natural cold or expeller pressed oils such as olive, soy, safflower, canola or sesame. Read the label carefully before buying. I like to put virgin olive oil over my baked potato, instead of salt-free butter. Also a little oil over baked beans and vegetables is great with a dash or spray of delicious Bragg Liquid Aminos. For variety try a sprinkle of kelp seasoning or parmesan cheese. We never use table salt.

The best way to eat potatoes is baked. I use a fast method of baking. Thoroughly scrub the potato (either white, yam or sweet). Do not wrap or oil it. Bake in 450° oven for 25 minutes. This converts the starch of the potato to a blood sugar. Be sure to eat the skin, too ... baked this fast way it's crunchy & delicious. We don't believe in microwaves. A safe, reasonable priced alternative is the convection oven. They're almost as fast as a microwave & they fit on your counter top.

Table salt has no place in your diet! Salt is an inorganic substance and only causes mischief in the body. Organic sodium from natural foods is the best. Read labels and if products contain added salt, do not buy them!

AVOID PROCESSED UNHEALTHY FOODS!

Eliminate refined white flour products and white sugar products entirely. No mushy, dead, refined cereals or those dry commercial cereals – for they are in a low rate of vibration, despite having been enriched with chemically produced vitamins and minerals. (Health food stores carry natural organic cereals if you desire a whole grain cereal.)

Avoid all these: • Fried foods • Frozen foods • Salted foods • Refined, preserved, chemicalized foods • Coffee, tea, cola drinks, alcohol, or sugared, salted juices • Over-cooked, over-salted vegetables, and salted creamed flour-thickened soups.

You now know the foods you can eat: fresh fruits, fresh juices, variety salads, fresh vegetables steamed, baked or wokked, vegetable proteins, fish, poultry, and, if you want, red meat – but do not eat it more than 2 to 3 times a week, and occasionally go 1 to 2 days a week on fruit only.

You now know the foods you cannot eat: refined, unhealthy processed, chemicalized foods & sugared beverages.

Use your imagination to plan enjoyable live food meals which are in a high rate of vibration. Above all, eat simply and occasionally go a full day on only fruits. Avoid too many mixtures; do not over-eat; be moderate in all things for the best of health. Eat only when you are really hungry, not because it is meal-time. Earn your food by activity, vigorous exercise and deep breathing. You will see how much more you enjoy your food when you deserve and earn your food!

THE MIRACLE POWER OF FRUIT

Always keep in mind that the most perfect food for man is fresh, ripe fruit. Nature, in her inimitable way, brings together in her fruits a marvelously-balanced, living combination of vital principles, in a high rate of vibration, bio-magnetized, to release the living building blocks so necessary for live body function.

Tinted by basking rays of vitalizing sun, breathing in draughts of magnetized air, drawing into itself vital minerals through its roots in the earth, delicious fruit is God's perfection . . . from His electro-chemical miracle laboratory!

Man can take all the chemicals of an apple out of a chemist's dish, but he cannot construct an apple! Man may analyze all the minerals of a cherry, but he does not even know what makes them red. He may take apart and try to reconstruct a grape, and find that the grape supports life and the broken-down chemicals do not!

Fruit contains certain bio-electric principles that give the electric spark of life. Fruit is the most perfect food of Nature and will support life indefinitely to a superior degree – when a body is cleansed and living in a natural environment.

Who has not had his mouth water when seeing a luscious dish of fruit before him – for instance a couple of yellow pears with a dash of pink or a beautiful bunch of tapering grapes, green or red or blue? The sight of fruit and the taste of it, more so, bring an abundant secretion of digestive juices, for they are natural foods of people. I can say without reserve that fruit is designed particularly well for our digestive tracts.

I have seen a sick person turn down all other food and drink a glass of freshly squeezed orange juice. His sick body craved the vital nutrients which are found in the ripe, juicy orange. I have seen children torn with fever ask for a glass of fruit juice. Why didn't they ask for a hot dog?

On the whole, fruit diets which consists solely of fruits are inefficient and impractical for the average American, although they would be splendid in a tropical climate. While man has come so far from his natural state that he cannot maintain an efficient standard as a fruitarian, still you need to *eat more fresh fruit!* One of the many reasons I love Hawaii – the luscious tropical fruits! Plan a Hawaiian vacation and enjoy the free Bragg Exercise Class. See details in front pages.

I especially recommend ripe bananas. Bananas are not a fattening fruit as is commonly supposed. They are 70% water and are extremely high in potassium. Apples of all kinds make excellent eating, as do pears and grapes. In the fall, winter and spring, eat organically grown dates, sun-dried figs, raisins and apricots along with fresh fruit. When you eat fruit, see how wonderful you feel and look!

The Miracle Food: The Avocado stands high as a miracle food of nature. The avocado tree is strong and insects do not bother it. It requires no spraying with poisonous chemicals. The avocado has a perfect balance of life-giving nutrients. It has an unsaturated fat which the body can handle perfectly. And they have even more potassium than bananas!

I eat avocados 3 to 4 times a week from my Santa Barbara ranch, where I grow three varieties of them. When they're ripe, I cut them in half, seed and peel them. After mashing them I add fresh mashed garlic (use a garlic press) and a dash of Bragg Liquid Aminos over them. Use sliced tomatoes, celery, carrot sticks, lettuce leaves, radish, cucumber and green bellpepper to dip into this "guacamole" for a delicious high vibration lunch.

FOODS IN A HIGH VIBRATION
CONTAIN LIFE-GIVING SUBSTANCE

When you eat only foods which are in a high vibration your body performs and operates by God's Universal Law and becomes a • Self-starting • Self-governing • Self-generating instrument! I want you to live by God's Laws of Nature and your body will be a fine working instrument for you at every age. If you have the desire to retain the vivacity, vitality, energy and enthusiasm of youth , the desire to turn back the clock of Father Time, when your bodies are bent, your eyes dimmed, your gait is halting – at an age when you should be buoyant with the spirit of youth, then I say: *there is but one way to live and that is Natures's Healthy Way!*

ENJOY A TIRELESS – AGELESS – PAINLESS BODY

Despite Calendar Years – with the Bragg Healthy Lifestyle

Inactive old people are unwanted, often by their families and society. Some are an encumbrance to themselves and everyone with whom they come in contact.

But do not despair in your golden years. My dad, Paul Bragg, said the 2nd half is best and can be the most fruitful years. Mother Teresa, Grandma Moses and Linus Pauling have proved that. Conrad Hilton and J.C. Penney, both Bragg Health Followers, lived strong, active lives to almost 99. And countless others have lived long and productive lives.

With the Bragg Healthy Lifestyle we teach you how to forget calendar years and to regain the vigor of your youth. You regain not only a youthful spirit, but much of the vigor of youth, and it is your duty to yourself to start today!

Square your shoulders and look life squarely in the face. Keep premature ageing out of your body by following the Bragg Healthy Lifestyle Blueprint. You must eat foods that have a high rate of vibration: an abundance of raw fruits and vegetables and include a water fast one day a week. Do deep breathing exercises, get 8 hours of restful sleep at night and keep your body relaxed. Don't let anything rob you of your emotional energy, nervous energy and Vital Force.*

Your body is being made new every day. Premature ageing and senility result from the debris that accumulates during the rebuilding process. Maintain proper body activity throughout every part of it, and there will be little or no buildup of debris that will clog & prematurely age your body.

Cultivate and hold onto the spirit of youth and it will be yours! You can feel younger! You can look younger! Keep your spine straight to maintain your energies at a high level. Follow the Bragg Healthy Lifestyle – miracles will follow!

If you are already in the clutches of premature ageing, begin now to fight for the return of youth. Work to restore this priceless possession.

*Read the Bragg book: *Building Powerful Nerve Force*. It's a life changer and shows you how to relieve stress, tensions and pressures naturally. See back pages for info.

46

Train your body as you would that of a race horse. Follow these clear, definite instructions, and you will gain strength, virility, energy, vivacity, enthusiasm, and make your life a daily enjoyment for the most precious of all earthly gifts – the power and joys of youthful, healthful living. Men and women have been young at 50, 60, 70, 80 and even 90. Some have retained the Spirit of Youth beyond the century mark.

Those who live in accordance with God's Universal Laws maintain that life grows more beautiful year by year; that its glories, its joys, its delights increase with age.

When you live the incomplete life, and give up the precious things of human existence for dietary excesses, for the pleasures of luxury and idleness, you are selling your birthright for a mess of potage.

Wake up to the possibilities within your reach! Rejuvenate your body. Make your mind keen and capable. Obey the Laws of Nature and you will achieve results that you now scarcely dare to dream.

SUGGESTIONS FOR A DAILY PROGRAM

Be sure you sleep in a thoroughly ventilated room so you get a large amount of oxygen while sleeping. Make sure your mattress is firm and flat. Sleep in a spread-out position to allow for good circulation. Do not sleep in a cramped position or sleep on your arm or shoulder. Spread out completely.

Oxygen is the life of the blood, and blood is the life of the body. A person weighing about 150 pounds, contains about 88 pounds of oxygen. Oxygen is the most important chemical of the body. Yet it is colorless, odorless and tasteless. Its main function is purification. Lack of oxygen in the body can lead to serious consequences. The majority of people are oxygen-starved because they are shallow breathers.*

To have a Youthful, Vital Life we need air in abundance, pure distilled water and plenty of fresh vegetables and fruits. Oxygen is an unquestionable source of indispensable energy necessary for higher vital activity in the human organism. It insures elimination, reconstruction and regeneration within the vital factors and metabolic activities of the physical body.

* Read the *Bragg Super Power Breathing Book* for Super Energy. See back pages for info.

Oxygen is an unquestionable source of indispensable energy necessary for higher vital activity in the human organism. It insures elimination, reconstruction and regeneration within the vital factors and metabolic activities of the physical body.

Through the function of the lungs, oxygen is absorbed, transformed and assimilated into the blood, bringing with it unknown factors in the vital forces of the atmosphere.

Plants – through their roots in the ground – absorb all the vital elements in the soil necessary for their life. If I cut or damage their roots, they die! Man's roots are his lungs.

We can only breathe adequately with sufficient physical movement. With the proper movements we are motivated to obtain the full elixir of life which is the breath of air. The stronger and more vigorous our movements, the more air we need and the greater is our rate of breath acceleration.

The oxygen in the air that we breathe dissolves and eliminates waste and builds the continuum of our cellular structure, thus maintaining our body to the highest degree possible. Each breath should detoxify and regenerate our vital forces. But, this must be supplemented completely by following the Bragg Healthy Lifestyle.

I want it definitely understood that both exercise and conscious deep breathing must be fortified with proper nutrition to prevent the degenerative process of the cells.

This explains why there is a decline of top athletes in their late twenties and thirties, who haven't consumed a correct nutritionally balanced diet. The average athlete reaches a peak at about 27 and then, sadly, begins to decline.

I know this to be true, as my father was an active athlete for over 75 years and we saw the finest athletes reach their peak and then slowly decline with many of them dying young.

Other Factors Affecting Breathing: Our thoughts and emotions interfere with our breathing. That is why, if we have a headache, or some other sudden symptom, a few minutes of deep conscious breathing exercises in the open air will help us detoxify and re-establish our internal balance.

Upon waking in the morning, stretch your legs and arms and body as you do when yawning. Continue this stretching process until you feel that every muscle has been properly and thoroughly awakened. Good circulation and elimination are the master keys to good health! That is the reason it is important to stretch and exercise your body. Do not do exercises just in the morning. Make some time during the day to keep your circulation strong throughout your cardio-vascular system during your waking hours. Do not sit longer than one hour at a time. Get up and move around.

To rest is to rust and rust is destruction! Don't sit in a car for more than an hour – stop the car and get out and stretch. Exercise your legs, body & do some deep breathing exercises.

EXERCISES HELP KEEP YOU
YOUTHFUL, FLEXIBLE AND FIT

You must fight off stiffness, if you want the body to feel youthful. Most prematurely old people find it impossible to straighten their spines or continually maintain good posture. Why? Because they have become stiff and rigid through lack of exercise and use.

It is no wonder that men and women become prematurely old, settle down and get crusty and *stiff-necked*. They don't do exercises that move their spinal joints! If you have already begun to acquire this stiffness, take warning now!

Go to Work on Yourself! The key to looking ten years younger is to keep your spine active, so strive for flexibility and elasticity in every part of your body, especially your spine! Youthful looking people have good postures.

The spine is a marvelous *instrument* as well as the central support of the whole body. It is made up of a flexible column of squarish bones which are joined together with rubbery puffs called discs. This wonderful piece of equipment stores its own lubrication in little sacs at the joints. The spine was designed for action! Keeping it loose and supple, and your whole body will move with grace, ease and youthfulness.

Healthy massages bring new changes to the body in many various forms: Unclogging of the body forces and machinery, promoting more circulation flowing, which brings more healing, new feelings and smoother muscular patterns that will in general bring you more vital health! Our inner and outer problems often hit us in the "gut" and muscles, and massage helps in this overall health practice. See pages 54-56 for more information.

49

AVOID THESE PROCESSED, REFINED, HARMFUL FOODS

Once you realize the irreparable harm caused to your body by refined, chemicalized, deficient foods, it is easy to eat correctly. Simply eliminate these "killer" foods from your diet and follow the Bragg Healthy Lifestyle. It provides the basic, essential nourishment your body needs to maintain you in super energy and health.

- Refined sugar or refined sugar products such as jams, jellies, preserves, marmalades, yogurts, ice cream, sherberts, Jello, cake, candy, cookies, chewing gum, soft drinks, pies, pastries, tapioca puddings, sugared fruit, juices & fruits canned in sugar syrup.

- Salted foods, such as corn chips, salted crackers, salted nuts.

- White rice & pearled barley.   • Fried & greasy foods.

- Commercial, highly processed dry cereals such as corn flakes, etc.

- Saturated fats & hydrogenated oils – enemies that clog bloodstream.

- Food which contains palm & cottonseed oil. Products labeled vegetable oil . . . find out what kind before you use it.

- Oleo & margarine . . . (saturated fats & hydrogenated oils).

- Peanut butter that contains hydrogenated, hardened oils.

- Coffee, decaffeinated coffee, China black tea & all alcoholic beverages.

- Fresh pork & pork products.   • Fried, fatty & greasy meats.

- Smoked meats, such as ham, bacon, sausage & smoked fish.

- Luncheon meats, hot dogs, salami, bologna, corned beef, pastrami & packaged meats containing dangerous sodium nitrate or nitrite.

- Dried fruits containing sulphur dioxide - a preservative.

- Do not eat chickens or turkeys that have been injected with stilbestrol, or fed with poultry feed that contains any drugs.

- Canned soups - read labels for sugar, starch, flour & preservatives.

- Food that contains benzoate of soda, salt, sugar, cream of tartar . . . & any additives, drugs or preservatives.

- White flour products such as white bread, wheat-white bread, enriched flours, rye bread that has wheat-flour in it, dumplings, biscuits, buns, gravy, noodles, pancakes, waffles, soda crackers, macaroni, spaghetti, pizza, ravioli, pies, pastries, cakes, cookies, prepared and commercial puddings and ready-mix bakery products. (Health Food Stores have huge varieties of 100% whole grain products – breads, crackers, pastas, pastries, etc.).

- Day-old cooked vegetables & potatoes & pre-mixed wilted salads.

- Pasteurized & filtered vinegars, malt & synthetic vinegars & distilled white vinegar. These are dead vinegars! *For info read Bragg Vinegar Book.*
(We use only organic, raw unfiltered Apple Cider Vinegar.)

FOOD AND PRODUCT SUMMARY

Today many of our foods are highly processed or refined, which robs them of essential nutrients, vitamins, minerals and enzymes; many contain harmful and dangerous chemicals. The research, findings and experience of top nutritionists, physicians and dentists have led them to discover that devitalized foods are a major cause of poor health, illness, cancer and premature death. The enormous increase in the last seventy years in degenerative diseases, such as heart disease, arthritis and dental decay substantiate this belief. Scientific research has shown that most of these afflictions can be prevented; and others, once established, may be arrested or even reversed through nutritional methods.

SUPER HEALTH WITH WHOLESOME, NATURAL FOOD

1. RAW FOODS: use food in its original state, organically grown whenever possible – especially fresh fruits, vegetables, whole grains, brown rice, beans, raw nuts and seeds.

2. VEGETABLE and ANIMAL PROTEIN:

   a. The legumes, soy and all other beans – *our favorites*.

   b. Nuts and seeds, raw and unsalted.

   c. Animal protein – variety meats, liver, kidney, brain, heart and poultry and seafood. Please eat sparingly but better yet try the healthy vegetarian diet. You can bake, roast, wok or broil your animal proteins. Eat them no more than 3 times a week if you must.

   d. Dairy products, eggs (fertile), unprocessed hard cheese and certified raw milk. (Personally we do not use milk and only occasionally unsalted butter and low or no-fat dairy yogurts.)

3. FRUITS and VEGETABLES: (organically grown is best – without the use of poisonous chemical sprays and fertilizers, – whenever possible); ask your market to stock organic produce. Steam, bake, saute or wok vegetables with distilled water, at low heat, for as short a time as possible.

4. 100% WHOLE GRAIN CEREALS, BREADS & FLOURS: they contain important B complex vitamins, vitamin E, minerals and the important unsaturated fatty acids.

5. COLD OR EXPELLER PRESSED VEGETABLE OILS: Olive, Canola, Sunflower and Sesame, etc. are excellent sources of the healthy essential unsaturated fatty acids, but use sparingly.

YOUR WAISTLINE IS YOUR LIFE-LINE, DATE-LINE AND HEALTH-LINE!

Get a tape measure and measure your waist. Write down the measurement. If you pursue vigorous abdominal and posture exercises combined with correct eating and a weekly 24 hour fast (and later on longer 3, 5 or 7 day fasts) in a short time you'll see a more trim and youthful waistline. *Trim waistlines can make people appear years younger* – now, let's get yours down to where it should be – if it's grown too big and fat. *It is a trim, lean horse for the long race of life.* I am sure we all want to be here for a long time! Living the Bragg Healthy Lifestyle is so wonderful. Each day is a precious gift to enjoy, treasure and guard for the healthy life is truly beautiful!

People abuse their abdomens abominably! You cannot eat dead, empty calorie foods and tell yourself that a tiny snack here and there won't show! You are completely wrong! Dead, devitalized foods create toxic poisons inside your body and this all helps to add flabby inches to the abdomen. Do not over-eat even the correct healthy foods, for your body only needs enough food (fuel) to maintain energy. When you stuff too much fuel into it, that's when you see fat people walking around . . . maybe you are one of them and you have over-fueled your body and are not burning up the excess.

You are not getting away with this kind of cheating – it's just cheating (hurting) yourself! Bear in mind as we live longer, the internal abdominal structure and stomach muscles relax more. This is called visceroptosis, or droopy tummy, and it is a common condition among older people who don't exercise those waist muscles. It can be a contributing cause of constipation, sluggish liver and even hernias.

When the abdominal wall becomes lazy and the consequent droop is compounded by a few layers of flab, trouble starts inside the abdomen. By the time most people have reached 40 they have a complete prolapsed abdomen. Start looking at people and you will notice what I'm saying is true!

So, don't let your abdomen droop, make every effort to bring it back to firmness again . . . it's amazing how quickly it responds to exercises and good posture.

Caution: The Army Diet – What you over-eat goes to the front.

A reminder: What's on the tablespoon becomes what's on the chair.

MAINTAIN YOUTHFUL POSTURE
FOR SUPER HEALTH

There is a fundamental relationship between good posture and youth on the one hand and bent posture and age on the other. To maintain the posture of youth actually means the maintenance of youth itself, because of the basic relationship between the healthy normal spine and bodily vigor: the condition which signifies youth, irrespective of how many years one has lived.

The most easily recognized sign of premature ageing is the forward bend of the spine, combined with the "round shoulders" which accompany it. Prematurely old people often exhibit this condition to a very marked degree, almost bending over double. Even schoolchildren sometimes display this sign of premature ageing. On the other hand, people of advanced years, by simply straightening their spines and walking erect, appear ten to thirty years younger than they really are. Look around you and start noticing postures and you will see what we mean!

One's entire life must be a constant fight to maintain the correct erect position. Remember: the spine is the fundamental structure of the human body. With the brain, in which it starts, it constitutes the center of the nervous system. All other parts of the body are, so to speak, appendages of the spine. If you did not have a spine, you would be a jellyfish, a shellfish, or an insect. Keep that spinal column straight, keep it flexible and keep it erect! Good health and longevity depends on a healthy erect body. Stretch up your spine, stand tall, sit tall, this gives your heart and organs room to operate more efficiently. Look at your posture in the mirror – then start improving it!

Bragg Posture Exercise – Tighten butt and suck in stomach muscles, lift up ribcage, stretch up spine, chest out, shoulders back, chin up slightly, line up straight (nose plumbline straight to belly button), drop hands to sides and swing to normalize your posture. Do this exercise often, miraculous changes will happen. You are retraining and strengthening your muscles to stand straight for health and youthfulness!

Ten little two-letter words of action
If it is to be, It is up to me!

The more natural food you eat, the more radiant health you will enjoy and you will be better able to promote the higher life of love and brotherhood. – Patricia Bragg

ALTERNATIVE HEALING THERAPIES
AND MASSAGE TECHNIQUES

Explore these wonderful natural methods of healing your body; then choose the technique that's best for your needs:

F. Mathius Alexander Technique — Lessons intended to end improper use of neuromuscular system and bring body posture back into balance. Eliminates psycho-physical interferences, helps release long-held tension, and aids in re-establishing muscle tone.

Chiropractic — Daniel David Palmer founded chiropractic in 1885 in Davenport, Iowa. From 16 schools now in the U.S., graduates are joining Health Practitioners in all the civilized nations of the world to share their health-healing techniques. Chiropractic is the largest healing profession and benefits millions. Treatment involves soft tissue, spinal and body adjustment to free the nervous system of interferences with normal body function. Its concern is the functional integrity of the muscular skeletal system. In addition to manual methods, chiropractors use physical therapy modalities, exercise, health and nutritional guidance.

Feldenkrais Method — Founded by Dr. Moshe Feldenkrais in late 1940s. Lessons lead to improved posture and help create ease and efficiency of movement. A great stress removal method.

Homeopathy — Developed by Dr. Samuel Hahnemann in the 1800s. Patients are treated with minute amounts of substances similar to those that cause a particular disease to trigger the body's own defenses. The homeopathic principle is *like cures like*. This safe and non-toxic remedy is #1 in Europe and Britain in alternative therapy because it's inexpensive, seldom has any side effects, and gets amazing, fast results.

Naturopathy — Brought to America by Dr. Benedict Lust, M.D., treatment utilizes diet, herbs, homeopathy, fasting, exercise, hydrotherapy, manipulation and sunlight. (Dr. Paul Bragg was a graduate of Dr. Lust's first Naturopathic School in the U.S.) Practitioners work with your body to naturally restore health, they reject surgery and drugs except as a last resort.

Osteopathy — The first School of Osteopathy was founded in 1892 by Dr. Andrew Taylor Still, M.D. There are now 15 such colleges in the U.S. Treatment involves soft tissue, spinal and body adjustments that free the nervous system from interferences which can cause illness. The complete system of healing by adjustment also includes good nutrition, physical therapies, proper breathing and good posture. Dr. Still's premise was that structure and function of the human body are interdependent and if the body structure is altered or abnormal, function is altered and illness results.

ALTERNATIVE HEALING THERAPIES
AND MASSAGE TECHNIQUES

Reflexology or Zone Therapy — Founded by Eunice Ingham, author of "The Story The Feet Can Tell," whose health career was inspired by a Bragg Health Crusade when she was 17. Relieves the body by removing crystalline deposits from meridians (nerve endings) of the feet by the therapist's using deep pressure massage. A form of Reflexology massage that has its early origins in China and is known to have been practiced by Kenyan natives and North American Indian tribes for centuries. Reflexology helps to activate the body's natural flow of energy by dislodging the collected deposits.

Reiki — A Japanese form of massage which means "Universal Life Energy." Reiki helps the body to detoxify then re-balance and heal itself. Discovered in the ancient Sutra manuscripts by Dr. Mikso Usui in 1822.

Rolfing — A technique developed by Ida Rolf in the 1930s in the U.S., variously called structural processing, postural release or structural dynamics. It is based on the concept that distortions of nominal function of organs and skeletal muscles occur throughout life and are accentuated by the effects of gravity on the body. Rolfing helps the individual to achieve balance and improved body posture. Methods involve the use of stretching, deep tissue massage and relaxation techniques to loosen old injuries and break bad movement patterns which cause long-term body stress.

Self Massage — Paul C. Bragg often said, "You can be your own best massage therapist, even if you have only one good hand." Near-miraculous improvements have been achieved by victims of accidents or strokes in bringing life back to afflicted parts of their own bodies by self-massage and even vibrators. Treatments can be day or night, almost continual. Also, self-massage can help achieve relaxation at day's end. Families and friends can learn and exchange massages; it's a wonderful sharing experience. Remember, babies also love and thrive with daily massages. Your family pets also love the soothing, healing touch of massage.

Aromatic Massage — It works two ways: The essence (smell) helps the patient relax as does the massage itself, while the massage is used to help absorption of essential natural oils used for centuries to treat numerous complaints. For example, Tiger Balm, Echinacea and Arnica help relieve muscle aches. Avoid creams and lotions with mineral oil because it clogs the skin's pores. Almond, avocado and olive oils are among the most popular. There are over 40 aromatics to use derived from herbs and other botanicals. (Pure rosemary oil, 6 drops to 6 ounces of almond oil, is a favorite.)

ALTERNATIVE HEALING THERAPIES
AND MASSAGE TECHNIQUES

Shiatsu — It means *finger pressure* in Japanese and is applied with pressure from the fingers, hands, elbows and even knees along the same 12 meridian paths used in acupuncture (note: use only disposable needles!), which has been used for centuries in the Orient to relieve pain, common ills and muscle stress and to aid lymphatic circulation. This is a form of acupuncture . . . acupressure without needle punctures.

Sports Massage — Developed over the years into a sophisticated, important support system for athletes, professional and amateur. Sports massage serves these functions, AMTA says: improving circulation and mobility to injured tissue, enabling athlete to recover more rapidly from myofascial injury, reducing muscle soreness and chronic strain patterns. Soft tissues are freed of trigger points and adhesions, thus contributing toward improvement of peak neuromuscular functioning and athletic performance. It's a preventive approach to injuries that can be suffered during training and it provides a psychological boost to athletes.

Tragering — Founded by Dr. Milton Trager M.D., who was inspired at age 18 by Paul C. Bragg to become a doctor. It is an experimental learning method which involves gentle shaking and rocking, suggesting a greater letting go, releasing tensions and lengthening of muscles for more body health. Tragering can do miraculous healing where needed in the muscles and entire body.

Water Therapy — Showers are wonderful. First apply almond, avocado, or olive oil to skin, then alternate hot and cold shower and massage needed areas while under shower. Garden hose massage is great in summer. Tub baths are wonderful as well: Apply oil and massage. For muscle aches, add 1 cup of apple cider vinegar or Epsom salts. Dry skin brushing (brush lightly) is wonderful for circulation, toning and healing. Also for variety use a loofah sponge for massaging in the shower and tub.

Swedish Massage — Oldest and most-used massage technique. Deep body massage that soothes, promotes circulation and is also a great way to loosen muscles before and after exercise.

Author's Comment: My father and I have personally sampled many of these techniques. In 1994 health care bills soared to over $980 billion, and it is estimated that by the year 2000 they will reach $1.7 trillion. It becomes more important than ever that we take responsibility for our own health. This includes seeking holistic health practitioners who are dedicated to keeping Americans well by inspiring them to practice prevention. Many alternative healing therapies are becoming popular – massage, color, aroma, sound-music, bio-feedback and yoga, to name a few. My advice to readers: *Explore them and be open to improving your earthly temple for a long, happy life. Seek and find the best for your body, mind and spirit.*   – Patricia Bragg

STOP DYING – START LIVING

The Bible tells us that *The Kingdom of Heaven is within us.* This statement we thoroughly believe. We can either make this body we live in a kingdom of heaven on earth or we can make it a torture chamber. It's all up to you.

After childhood, the kind of body you live in is strictly up to you! We cannot live your life for you. Nor can anyone else! You are a mature adult, and you must face the reality of life. We are sure you have the will power and desire to follow the Bragg Healthy Lifestyle – so start today!

This is a Master Blueprint to greater Physical Perfection because it works with the Laws of God and Nature, and they make no compromises! You either follow them or you break them! You cannot break a natural law or a God law – for it only breaks you sooner or later in your foolish attempt!

FOLLOW THESE NATURAL LAWS FOR PHYSICAL PERFECTION

These Laws God put in motion are Perfect Laws created for your own good:

- You must eat Natural Foods.
- You must breathe deeply of God's air.
- You must exercise the 640 muscles of your body.
- You must give your body pure, clean water.*
- You must give your body sunshine (sunbaths).
- You must not over-work your body; this leads to stress, strains, tensions and nerve depletion.
- You must keep the body clean outside and inside.
- You must live by divine intelligence and wisdom.

We are creatures of a Perfect Creator. Inherent within us is the potential to become more physically perfect. It must be the intent of our Perfect Creator to have us physically perfect for a healthy, happy, and peaceful life!

Whe we are not physically perfect we are out of harmony with the Creator's design, and therefore out of harmony with God's intent, will and law. In simpler words, we are, in our living habits, opposing the will of God.

---

* Read the Bragg Book *The Shocking Truth About Water* for reasons you should drink pure, distilled water – a must reading! See back pages to order.

So, you see that to reach physical perfection we must live on all four planes: *The Physical, The Mental, The Emotional and The Spiritual.* By living on the physical plane correctly we will reach a higher mental, emotional and spiritual state.

If you eat God and Nature's foods and build a healthy red clean bloodstream you are going to be keener mentally. And the wonderful part of living by God and Nature's Blueprint – is we find a new calmness coming over us. You'll experience a new feeling of confidence, of peace and serenity. When every cell, organ and body part are functioning perfectly, the body becomes more perfect physically, mentally and spiritually. What complete satisfaction you will feel when you are living this Bragg Healthy Lifestyle and reaping the great rewards!

Your degree of physical perfection is the measure of your efforts in cooperating (by daily proper foods, exercise, deep breathing and youthful thinking) with your Creator's design or intent, that you become and remain physically healthy, youthful, active and of service – regardless of your age.

THE BODY MUST OBEY YOUR MIND

Flesh is dumb! You can put anything in your stomach from pickles to hot dogs. It is not the stomach that rules the body, it is an intelligent and reasoning mind. Let me close this Bragg Healthy Lifestyle Blueprint with the unequivocal statement that the properly directed mind can make the body follow the Bragg Healthy Lifestyle, therefore helping in making the body more physically perfect.

And this is our goal for you – Radiant, Super Health.

Blessings for Health, Peace, Joy, Vitality Supreme and Long-Lasting Youthfulness . . . With Love,

Patricia Bragg

"Open thou mine eyes, that I may behold wondrous things out of thy law." – Psalms 119:18

Nutrition directly affects growth, development, reproduction, well-being of an individual's physical and mental condition. Health depends upon nutrition more than on any other single factor. – Dr. Wm. H. Sebrell, Jr.

HEALTHY HEART HABITS FOR A LONG, VITAL LIFE

Live foods make live people, and you are what you eat, drink and do, so eat a low-fat, low-sugar, high-fiber diet of whole grains and pastas, beans, brown rice, fresh salad greens, sprouts, vegetables, fruits, raw seeds, nuts, juices and six to eight glasses of distilled water daily.

Earn your food with daily exercise, for regular exercise improves your health, heart, flexibility and endurance, and helps open the cardiovascular system. Only 45 minutes a day can do miracles for your mind and body. You become revitalized with new zest for living.

We are made of tubes. To help keep them clean and open, make a mixture using 1/2 raw oat bran and 1/2 psyllium husk powder and add 1 to 3 tsp daily to juices, pep drinks, herb teas, soups, hot cereals, foods, etc. Daily I also take one Cayenne capsule (40,000 HU) daily a meal.

Another way to daily guard against clogged tubes is to add 2 Tbsp soy lecithin granules [fat emulsifier] to beverages, veggies, soups, etc.

Take 50 to 100 mgs regular-released Niacin (B-3) with one meal daily to help cleanse and open the cardiovascular system. Skin flushing may occur, nothing to worry about as it shows it's working! After cholesterol level reaches 180 or lower, take one to two Niacin weekly.

Your heart needs a good balance of nutrients, so take a natural vitamin-mineral food supplement with extra Vitamin E (mixed Tocopherols), Vitamin C, Magnesium, Selenium, Zinc, Beta Carotene & the amino acid L-Carnitine – your heart's super helpers! It's also wise to take a multi-digestant enzyme with each meal to aid digestion.

Also use the amazing antioxidants Pycnogenol (grape seeds)or SOD (super oxide dismutase). They help flush out dangerous free radicals that can cause havoc with your cardiovascular pipes and general health. Latest research shows they promote longevity, slow ageing, fights toxins, age spots, arthritis and its stiffness, swelling and pain, and help prevent cataracts, jet lag, exhaustion and disease.

Count your blessings daily while you do your 30 minutes or more brisk walk and exercises with these affirmations – *health! strength! youth! vitality! peace! laughter! humility! understanding! forgiveness! joy!* and *love for eternity!*– and soon all these qualities will come flooding and bouncing into your life. With blessings of super health, peace and love to you, our dear friends and readers. – Patricia Bragg

RECOMMENDED BLOOD CHEMISTRY VALUES

- Total Cholesterol: 180 mg/dl or less; 150 mg/dl or less is optimal
- Total Cholesterol, Childhood Years: 140 mg/dl or less
- HDL Cholesterol: Men, 46 mg/dl or more; Women, 56 mg/dl or more
- HDL Cholesterol Ratio: 3.2 or less • Glucose: 80-100 mg/dl
- Triglycerides: 100 mg/dl or less • LDL Cholesterol: 120 or less

We admire everyone who exercises and keeps healthy and fit.

IRON PUMPING OLDSTERS (86 to 96) TRIPLE THEIR MUSCLE STRENGTH IN U.S. STUDY

WASHINGTON, June 13, 1990 – Ageing nursing home residents, in Boston study, "pumping iron"? Elderly weight-lifters tripling and quadrupling their muscle strength? Is it possible? Most people would doubt? and wonder? Government experts on ageing gave those questions a resounding "yes" with the results of this new study.

They turned a group of frail Boston nursing-home residents, aged 86 to 96, into weight-lifters to demonstrate that it's never too late to reverse age-related declines in muscle strength. The group participated in a regimen of high-intensity weight-training in a study conducted by the Agriculture Department's Human Nutrition Research Center on Ageing at Tufts University in Boston. "A high-intensity weight training program is capable of inducing dramatic increases in muscle strength in frail men and women up to 96 years of age," reported Dr. Maria A. Fiatarone, who headed the study.

Amazing Health & Strength Results in 8 Weeks

"The favorable response to strength training in our subjects was remarkable in light of their very advanced age, extremely sedentary habits, multiple chronic diseases, functional disabilities and nutritional inadequacies. The elderly weight-lifters increased their muscle strength by anywhere from three-fold to four-fold in as little as eight weeks. Fiatarone said they probably were stronger at the end of the program than they had been in years!

Fiatarone and her associates emphasized the safety of such a closely supervised weight-lifting program, even among people in frail health. The average age of the 10 participants, for instance, was 90. Six had coronary heart disease; seven had arthritis; six had bone fractures resulting from osteoporosis; four had high blood pressure; and all had been physically inactive for years. Yet no serious medical problems resulted from the program, only good!

A few of the participant did report minor muscle and joint aches, but 9 of the 10 completed the program. One man, aged 86, felt a pulling sensation at the site of a previous hernia incision and dropped out after four weeks.

The study participants, drawn from a 712 bed long-term care facility in Boston, worked out 3 times a week. They performed 3 sets of 8 repetitions with each leg on a weight-lifting machine. The weights were gradually increased from about 10 pounds initially to about 40 pounds at the end of the eight-week program.

Fiatarone said the study carries important implications for older people, on improving their wellness and fitness, who represent a growing proportion of the U.S. population. A decline in muscle strength and size is the more predictable feature of ageing.

60

EXERCISE KEEPS
YOU YOUNGER,
HEALTHIER

PAUL C. BRAGG
WEIGHTLIFTS
3 TIMES A WEEK

Muscle strength in the average adult decreases by 30 percent to 50 percent during the course of life. Experts on ageing do not know whether the decrease is an unavoidable consequence of ageing or results mainly from sedentary life-style and other controllable factors.

Muscle atrophy and weakness is not merely a cosmetic problem in elderly people, especially the frail elderly. Researchers have lined muscle weakness with recurrent falls, a major cause of immobility and death in the American elderly population. This is causing millions of dollars yearly in staggering medical costs.

Previous studies have suggested that weight training can be helpful in reversing age-related muscle weakness. But Fiatarone said physicians have been reluctant to recommend weight-lifting for frail elderly with multiple health problems. This new government study might be changing their minds. Also, this study shows the great importance of keeping the 640 muscles as active and fit as possible to maintain general good health.

HEALTHY BEVERAGES
Fresh Juices, Herbal Teas and Pep Drinks

These freshly squeezed vegetable and fruit juices are important to the Bragg Healthy Lifestyle. We feel it's not wise to drink beverages with your main meals. But if during the day you wish a glass of freshly squeezed orange, grapefruit, vegetable juice, Bragg Vinegar Drink, herb tea or try a hot cup of Bragg Liquid Aminos Broth (1/2 to 1 tsp Bragg Liquid Aminos in cup of hot distilled water) . . . these are all ideal pick-me-up beverages.

The Bragg Favorite Juice Cocktail – This drink consists of all raw vegetables (please – organic when possible) which we prepare in our vegetable juicer: Carrots, Celery, Beets, Cabbage, Watercress and Parsley. The great purifier Garlic is optional.

The Bragg Favorite Health "Pep" Drink – After our morning exercises often we enjoy this instead of fruit. It's also delicious and powerfully nutritious as a meal anytime: lunch, dinner or to take in a thermos to work, school, to the park or hiking, etc.

BRAGG HEALTHY PEP DRINK

Prepare the following in blender, add 1 ice cube if desired colder:

Choice of: freshly squeezed orange juice; carrot and greens juice; unsweetened pineapple juice; or 1-1/2 cups distilled water with:

1/2 tsp raw wheat germ	1/4 tsp Vitamin C powder
1/3 tsp flax seed oil, optional	1/4 tsp nutritional yeast flakes
1/4 tsp green powder (barley, etc.)	1 to 2 bananas, ripe
1/2 tsp raw oat bran	1 tsp raw honey, optional
1/2 tsp psyllium husk powder	1 tsp soy protein powder
1/2 tsp lecithin granules	1 tsp raw sunflower seeds

Optional: 4 apricots (sundried, unsulphured). Soak in jar overnight in distilled water or unsweetened pineapple juice. We soak enough to last for several days. Keep refrigerated. In summer you can add fresh fruit in season: peaches, strawberries, berries, apricots, etc. instead of the banana. In winter add apples, oranges, pears or persimmons or try sugar-free, frozen fruits. Serves 1 to 2.

Patricia's Delicious Health Popcorn

Use freshly popped popcorn (my favorite is the non-oil, air popped). If desired, use olive, soy, or canola oil, or melted salt-free butter. Add several dashes or sprays of Bragg's Liquid Aminos to the oil and pour over popcorn. Sprinkle with nutritional yeast flakes or grated parmesan cheese. For variety, add a pinch of Italian herbs, cayenne pepper, mustard powder or fresh crushed garlic to the liquid mixture.

Fasting is the greatest remedy; the physician within. – Paracelsus
15th century physician who established the role of chemistry in medicine.

BRAGG FAMOUS RAW VEGETABLE GARDEN SALAD

2 *stalks celery, sliced*	1/3 *cup red cabbage, chopped*
1/4 *diced bellpepper & seeds*	1/2 *c alfalfa or sunflower sprouts*
1/4 *cucumber, sliced*	1 *raw beet, grated*
3 *med. tomatoes*	1 *carrot, grated*
2 *spring onions with tops*	1 *turnip, grated*
1/2 *cup green cabbage, sliced*	1 *avocado (ripe)*

For variety add raw zucchini, sugar peas, mushrooms, broccoli, cauliflower. Dice avocado & tomato, & serve on side as a dressing. Chop, slice or grate vegetables fine to medium for variety in size. Mix vegetables thoroughly and serve on a bed of lettuce, spinach, watercress or chopped cabbage. Serve choice of fresh squeezed lemon, orange or dressing separately. Chill salad plates in freezer before serving. Always eat your salad first before serving hot dishes. Serves 3 to 5.

DELICIOUS VINAIGRETTE HEALTH DRESSING

1/2 *c apple cider vinegar*	1/3 *tsp Bragg Liquid Aminos*
1 to 2 *tsp raw honey*	1 to 2 *cloves garlic, minced*

1/3 *c virgin olive oil, or blend with canola, soy or sesame*
1 *tbsp fresh herbs, minced or pinch Italian dry herbs*

Combine ingredients in jar, blend and refrigerate.

For delicious herbal vinegar: in quart jar add 1/2 cup tightly packed, crushed fresh sweet basil, tarragon, dill, oregano, or any fresh herbs desired, combined or singly. (If *dried* herbs, use 1 to 2 tsp herbs.) Add apple cider vinegar, store two weeks in warm place, then strain and refrigerate.

VINAIGRETTE – HONEY – CELERY SEED DRESSING

1/4 *tsp dry mustard*	1/3 *cup apple cider vinegar*
1/4 *tsp Bragg Aminos*	2 *tbsp virgin olive oil*
1/4 *tsp paprika*	1 *medium onion, minced*
3 *tbsp raw honey*	1/2 *tsp celery seed*

Blend ingredients in blender or jar, then last add onion and celery seed and blend lightly. Refrigerate in covered jar.

Healthy, healing dietary fibers are fresh vegetables, fresh fruits, salads and whole grains and their products. These health builders help to normalize blood pressure, cholesterol and promote healthy elimination.

Living under conditions of modern life, it is important to bear in mind that the refinement, over processing & cooking of food products either entirely eliminates or in part destroys the vital elements in the original material.
– United States Department of Agriculture

FOOD FOR THOUGHT

Fruit bears the closest relation to light. The sun pours a continuous flood of light into the fruits, and they furnish the best portion of food a human being requires for the sustenance of mind and body. — Alcott

The purest food is fruit, next the cereals, then the vegetables. All pure poets have abstained almost entirely from animal food. Especially should a minister take less meat when he has to write a sermon. The less meat the better sermon. — A. Bronson Alcott

There is much false economy: those who are too poor to have seasonable fruits and vegetables, will yet have pie and pickles all the year. They cannot afford oranges, yet can afford tea and coffee daily. — Health Calendar

The men who kept alive the flame of learning and piety in the Middle Ages were mainly vegetarians. — Sir William Axon

Hearty foods are those in which there is an abundance of potential energy.

If families could be induced to substitute the apple — sound, ripe, and luscious — for the white sugar, whiteflour pies, cakes, candies, and other sweets with which children are too often stuffed, there would be a diminution of doctors' bills, sufficient in a single year to lay up a stock of this delicious fruit for a season's use.

To maintain good health the body must be exercised properly [walking, jogging, deep breathing, good posture, etc.], and nourished wisely [natural foods], so as to provide and increase the good life of joy and happiness. — Paul C. Bragg

The lightest breakfast is the best. — Oswald

DO MORE THAN
1. Do more than preach, practice.
2. Do more than think, ponder.
3. Do more than sympathize, empathize.
4. Do more than scold, set an example.
5. Do more than criticize, praise.
6. Do more than dream, struggle to make it reality.

— Rev. Paul Osumi, Honolulu

FROM THE AUTHORS

GO ORGANIC

This book was written for You. It can be your passport to the Good Life. We Professional Nutritionists join hands in one common objective – a high standard of health for all and many added years to your life. Scientific Nutrition points the way – Nature's Way – the only lasting way to build a body free of degenerative diseases and premature aging. This book teaches you how to work with Nature, not against her. Doctors, nurses, and professional care givers who care for the sick try to repair depleted tissues, which too often mend poorly – if at all. Many of them praise the spreading of this new scientific message of natural foods and methods for long-lasting health and youthfulness at any age. To speed the spreading of this tremendous message, this book was written.

Statements in this book are recitals of scientific findings, known facts of physiology, biological therapeutics and reference to ancient writings as they are found. Paul C. Bragg practiced the natural methods of living for over 80 years with highly beneficial results, knowing that they were safe and of great value. His daughter Patricia Bragg worked with him to carry on the Health Crusade. They make no specific claims regarding the effectiveness of these methods for any individual, and assume no obligation for any opinions expressed in this book.

No cure for disease is offered in this book. No foods or diets are offered for the treatment or cure of any specific ailment. Nor is it intended as, or to be used as, literature aimed at promoting any food product. Paul C. Bragg and Patricia Bragg express their opinions solely as Public Health Educators, Professional Nutritionists and Teachers.

Experts may disagree with some of the statements made in this book, particularly those pertaining to nutritional recommendations. However, any such statements are considered to be factual, based upon the long-time experience of Paul C. Bragg and Patricia Bragg. If you suspect you have a medical problem, please seek alternative health professionals to help you make the healthiest and wisest informed choices.

BRAGG BLESSINGS FROM OUR HOME

From the Bragg home to your home we share our years of health knowledge – years of living close to God and Nature and what joys of fruitful, radiant living this produces – this my Father and I share with you and your loved ones. With Love and Blessings for Health and Happiness,

Patricia Bragg

Take time
for **12** things

1 Take time to Work—
it is the price of success.

2 Take time to Think—
it is the source of power.

3 Take time to Play—
it is the secret of youth.

4 Take time to Read—
it is the foundation of knowledge.

5 Take time to Worship—
it is the highway of reverance and washes the
dust of earth from our eyes.

6 Take time to Help and Enjoy Friends—
it is the source of happiness.

7 Take time to Love—
it is the one sacrament of life.

8 Take time to Dream—
it hitches the soul to the stars.

9 Take time to Laugh—
it is the singing that helps with life's loads.

10 Take time for Beauty—
it is everywhere in nature.

11 Take time for Health—
it is the true wealth and treasure of life.

12 Take time to Plan—
it is the secret of being able to have time to
take time for the first eleven things.

YOUR BIRTHRIGHT
HEALTH
CULTIVATE IT

*"Teach me Thy way, O Lord;
and Lead me in a plain path . . . "*
Psalms 97:11

Exercise for Health

BRAGG HEALTHY LIFESTYLE
FOR A LIFETIME OF SUPER HEALTH

In a broad sense, "Bragg Healthy Lifestyle for the Total Person" is a combination of physical, mental, emotional, social, and the spiritual components. The ability of the individual to function effectively in his environment depends on how smoothly these components function as a whole. Of all the qualities that comprise an integrated personality, a totally healthy, fit body is one of the most desirable...so start today for achieving your health goals!

A person may be said to be totally physically fit if he functions as a total personality with efficiency and without pain or discomfort of any kind. This is to have a Painless, Tireless, Ageless body, possessing sufficient muscular strength and endurance to maintain a healthy posture and successfully carry on the duties imposed by life and the environment, to meet emergencies satisfactorily and have enough energy for recreation and social obligations after the "work day" has ended. It is to meet the requirements for his environment through possessing the resilience to recover rapidly from fatigue, tension, stress and strain of daily living without the aid of stimulants, drugs or alcohol, and enjoy natural recharging sleep at night and awaken fit and alert in the morning for the challenges of the new fresh day ahead.

Keeping the body totally healthy and fit is not a job for the uninformed or the careless person. It requires an understanding of the body and of a healthy lifestyle and then following that lifestyle for a long, happy life. The result of the "Bragg Healthy Lifestyle" is to wake up the possibilities within you, rejuvenate your body, mind and soul to total balanced health...It's within your reach, so don't procrastinate, start today! Our hearts go out to touch your heart with nourishing, caring love for your total health.

Patricia Bragg and Paul C. Bragg

Dear friend, I wish above all things that thou may prosper and be in health even as the soul prospers. - 3 John 2

67

Is everything you do
a big effort?

•

Have you started to lose
your skin-tone?
Muscle-tone?

•

Do small things irritate you?
Are you forgetful?
Confused?

•

Have voices begun to fade?

•

Has your vision started to dim?

•

Do you wobble a little
when you walk?

•

Do you get out of breath
when you climb stairs?

•

How limber is your back?

•

Do your joints creak?

•

How well do you adjust
to cold and heat?

•

Ask yourself this important question:
Do I seem to be slipping and
not quite like myself anymore?
If the answer to this question is "Yes"
You had better do something about it.

START TODAY...
living the
Bragg
Healthy
Lifestyle!

68

PATRICIA BRAGG N.D., Ph.D.
Angel of Health & Healing
Author, Lecturer, Nutritionist, Health Educator & Fitness Advisor to World Leaders, Hollywood Stars, Singers, Dancers & Athletes

Daughter of the world renowned health authority, Paul C. Bragg, Patricia Bragg has won international fame on her own in this field. She conducts Health and Fitness Seminars for Women's, Men's, Youth and Church Groups throughout the world... and promotes Bragg "How-To, Self-Health" Books in Lectures, on Radio and Television Talk Shows throughout the English-speaking world. Consultants to Presidents and Royalty, to the Stars of Stage, Screen and TV and to Champion Athletes, Patricia and her father are Co-Authors of the Bragg Health Library of Instructive, Inspiring Books that promotes the Bragg Healthy Lifestyle for a longer, vital, healthier life!

Patricia herself is the symbol of health, perpetual youth and super energy. She is a living and sparkling example of her and her father's healthy lifestyle precepts and this she loves sharing world-wide.

A fifth generation Californian on her mother's side, Patricia was reared by the Bragg Natural Health Method from infancy. In school, she not only excelled in athletics, but also won honors for her studies and her counseling. She is an accomplished musician and dancer... as well as tennis player and mountain climber... and the youngest woman ever to be granted a U.S. Patent. Patricia is a popular gifted Health Teacher and a dynamic, in-demand Talk Show Guest where she spreads the simple, easy-to-follow Bragg Healthy Lifestyle for everyone of all ages.

Man's body is his vehicle through life, his earthly temple ... and the creator wants us filled with joy & health for a long fruitful life. The Bragg Crusades of Health and Fitness (3 John 2) has carried her around the world over 10 times – spreading physical, spiritual, emotional, mental health and joy. Health is our birthright and Patricia teaches how to prevent the destruction of our health from man-made wrong habits of living.

Patricia's been Health Consultant to American Presidents and British Royalty, to Betty Cuthbert, Australia's "Golden Girl," who holds 16 world records and four Olympic gold medals in women's track and to New Zealand's Olympic Track and Triathlete Star, Allison Roe. Among those who come to her for advice are some of Hollywood's top Stars from Clint Eastwood to the ever-youthful singing group, The Beach Boys and their families, Singing Stars of the Metropolitan Opera and top Ballet Stars. Patricia's message is of world-wide appeal to people of all ages, nationalities and walks-of-life. Those who follow the Bragg Health Books and attend the Bragg Crusades World-wide are living testimonials like ageless, super athlete, Jack LaLanne, who at age 15 went from sickness to Total Health!

Patricia Bragg inspires you to Renew, Rejuvenate & Revitalize your life with the "Bragg Healthy Lifestyle" Seminars and Lectures worldwide. These events are life changing, where millions have benefited with a longer, healthier life! She would love to share with your community, organization, church groups, etc. Also, she is a perfect radio and T.V. talk show guest to spread the message of health and fitness in your area.

Write or call (805) 968-1020 for requests and information:
HEALTH SCIENCE, BOX 7, SANTA BARBARA, CA 93102, USA

PAUL C. BRAGG N.D., Ph.D.

Life Extension Specialist • World Health Crusader
Lecturer and Advisor to Olympic Athletes, Royalty and Stars
Originator of Health Food Stores – Now Worldwide

For almost a Century, Living Proof that his
"Health and Fitness Way of Life" Works Wonders!

Paul C. Bragg is the Father of the Health Movement in America. This dynamic Crusader for worldwide health and fitness is responsible for more *firsts* in the history of Health than any other individual.

Here are Bragg's amazing pioneering achievements the world now enjoys:

- Bragg originated, named and opened the first *Health Food Store* in America.
- Bragg Crusades pioneered the first Health Lectures across America, inspiring followers to open health stores in cities across the land and now worldwide.
- Bragg introduced pineapple juice and tomato juice to the American public.
- He was the first to introduce and distribute honey nationwide.
- He introduced Juice Therapy in America by importing the first hand-juicers.
- Bragg pioneered Radio Health Programs from Hollywood three times daily.
- Paul and Patricia pioneered a Health TV show from Hollywood to spread *Health and Happiness*... the name of the show! It included exercises, health recipes, visual demonstrations, & guest appearances by famous, health-minded people.
- He created the first health foods and products and made them available nationwide: herb teas, health beverages, seven-grain cereals and crackers, health cosmetics, health candies, calcium, vitamins and mineral supplements, wheatgerm, digestive enzymes from papaya, herbs & kelp seasonings, amino acids from soybeans. He inspired others to follow and now thousands of health items are available worldwide.
- He opened the first health restaurants and the first health spas in America.

Crippled by TB as a teenager, Bragg developed his own eating, breathing and exercising program to rebuild his body into an ageless, tireless, pain-free citadel of glowing, radiant health. He excelled in running, swimming, biking, progressive weighttraining and mountain climbing. He made an early pledge to God, in return for his renewed health, to spend the rest of his life showing others the road to health. He honored his pledge! Bragg's health pioneering made a difference worldwide.

A living legend and beloved counselor to millions, Bragg was the inspiration and personal advisor on diet and fitness to top Olympic Stars from 4-time swimming Gold Medalist Murray Rose to 3-time track Gold Medalist Betty Cuthbert of Australia, his relative Don Bragg (pole-vaulting Gold Medalist), and countless other champions. Jack LaLanne, the original TV King of Fitness, says, *Bragg saved my life at age 15 when I attended the Bragg Crusade in Oakland, California.* From the earliest days, Bragg was advisor to the greatest Hollywood Stars and to giants of American Business. J. C. Penney, Del E. Webb and Conrad Hilton are just a few who he inspired to long, successful, healthy, active lives!

Dr. Bragg changed the lives of millions worldwide in all walks of life with the Bragg Health Crusades, Books, Tapes, Radio and TV appearances.

HEALTH SCIENCE, Box 7, SANTA BARBARA, CA 93102 USA

BRAGG "HOW-TO, SELF-HEALTH" BOOKS

Authored by America's First Family of Health

Live Longer – Healthier – Stronger Self-Improvement Library

Qty.	Bragg Book Titles Order Form Health Science ISBN 0-87790	Price	$ Total
____	**Vegetarian** Gourmet Health **Recipes** (no salt, no sugar, yet delicious)	7.95	•
____	**Bragg's Complete Gourmet Recipes** for Vital Health – 448 pages	8.95	•
____	The **Miracle of Fasting** (Bragg Bible of Health for physical rejuvenation)	7.95	•
____	Bragg **Health & Fitness Manual** for All Ages — Swim-Bike-Run		
	A Must for Athletes, Triathletes & would-be-athletes – 600 pages	16.95	•
____	Build Powerful **Nerve Force** (reduce stress, fear, anger, worry).	5.95	•
____	Keep Your **Heart & Cardio-Vascular System** Healthy & Fit at Any Age	5.95	•
____	The Natural Way to **Reduce** (lose 10 pounds in 10 days)	6.95	•
____	The Shocking Truth About **Water** (learn safest water to drink & why)	5.95	•
____	Your Health and Your **Hair**, Nature's Way to Beautiful Hair (easy-to-do method) .	6.95	•
____	**Healthful Eating** Without Confusion (removes doubt & questions)	5.95	•
____	**Sauerkraut Recipes** Raw, Salt-Free (learn to make your own – it's so healthy) .	2.95	•
____	Nature's Healing System to **Improve Eyesight** in 90 days (foods, exercises, etc.)	6.95	•
____	**Super Power Breathing** for Super Health, High Energy & Longevity	6.95	•
____	**Building Strong Healthy Feet** — Complete Healthy Foot Program	6.95	•
____	**Toxicless Diet-Purification** & Healing System **(Stay Ageless Program)**	5.95	•
____	**Apple Cider Vinegar Miracles** – Health System	5.95	•
____	**Fitness/Spine Motion** — For More Flexible, Pain-free Back	3.95	•
____	**Nature's Way to Health** (simple method for long, healthy life)	5.95	•

☐	**Total Copies**	Prices subject to change without notice.	**TOTAL BOOKS** $	•

	CA residents add sales tax	•
Shipping: Please add $2.00 for first book, $1.00 for each additional. Add $3.50 each for rush. USA retail book orders over $35.00 add $5.00 only. Canada add $3.00 per book. Foreign orders add $4.00 per book.	**Shipping & Handling**	•
	TOTAL ENCLOSED (USA Funds Only) $	•

Please Specify: ☐ Money Order   ☐ Cash   ☐ Check

Charge To: ☐ Visa   ☐ Master Card   ☐ Discover   month   year

Credit Card Number: _ _ _ _ _ _ _ _ _ _ _ _ _ _ _ _   Card Expires: ____ | ____

MasterCard   VISA   DISCOVER   **Signature:** _____

CREDIT CARD ORDERS ONLY
CALL **(800) 446-1990**
OR FAX **(805) 968-1001**

Business office calls (805) 968-1020 We accept MasterCard Discover or VISA phone orders. Please prepare your order using this order form. It will speed your call and serve as your order record. Hours: 9 to 4 pm Pacific Time, Monday thru Thursday.
To order online visit our Web site: http://www.bragg.com

Mail to: **HEALTH SCIENCE, Box 7, Santa Barbara, CA 93102 U.S.A.**

Please Print or Type – Be sure to give street & house number to facilitate delivery

BOF-950

Name	
Address	Apt. No.
City	State
( ) Phone	Zip

Bragg Books available most Health & Book Stores – Nationwide

SEND FOR IMPORTANT HEALTH BULLETINS

Let Health Science send you, your relatives and friends the latest News Bulletins on Health and Nutrition Discoveries. These are sent periodically. Please enclose one dollar for each USA name listed to cover postage and printing. Foreign listings please send international postal reply coupons. Print or type addresses, thank you.

HEALTH SCIENCE Box 7, Santa Barbara, California 93102 USA

●
_____
Name

               (   )
_____
Address   Phone

_____
City   State   Zip Code

●
_____
Name

               (   )
_____
Address   Phone

_____
City   State   Zip Code

●
_____
Name

               (   )
_____
Address   Phone

_____
City   State   Zip Code

●
_____
Name

               (   )
_____
Address   Phone

_____
City   State   Zip Code

●
_____
Name

               (   )
_____
Address   Phone

_____
City   State   Zip Code